BEING IN MY OWN WAY

A GUIDED REFLECTION ON BECOMING MORE INTENTIONAL

RICHARD INGRAM

UNLABELED PRESS

http://unlabeled.press | inquiry@unlabeled.press

Copyright © 2023 by Richard Ingram | hello@richardingram.me

All images used with permission. Unless captioned otherwise, all images used in essays were generated by the author with Dall-E or Midjourney.

All rights reserved.

No portion of this book may be reproduced in any form without written permission from the publisher or author, except as permitted by U.S. copyright law.

To request permission, contact hello@richardingram.me

Paperback: 978-1-962579-00-1
Ebook: 978-1-962579-01-8
Audiobook: 978-1-962579-02-5

Contents

Epigraph	VII
Letter to the Reader	VIII
Introduction	1
Part One	3
Values	4
DIMTY	6
WMM	7
Understanding and Compassion	9
Be curious, be kind, be whole, do good things.	10
Mindset	13
Blind Men and the Elephant	14
Pets of the Mind	19
System 1 and System 2	24
Availability Bias	27
Part Two	29
1. Walter	30
2. Labels	33

3. Curiosity   36

4. Coins   38

5. Seeing   41

6. Unfinished   43

7. Fooling   46

8. The Letter   48

9. Remote Start   50

10. Socks   52

11. Haunted   54

12. Shadows   56

13. Murder   58

14. Grand Theft Auto   60

15. Stairs   62

16. Jokes   64

17. Crossroads   67

18. Walking   69

19. Chewie   71

20. Corners   74

21. Farmers   76

22. M&Ms   78

23. Change   80

24. Oatmeal   82

25. Sewing   84

26. Ghost Stories	86
27. Inviting	89
28. Different	91
29. Pistol Shrimp	93
30. Ping	95
31. Learning	97
32. Mood	99
33. Wrecked	102
34. Oh Well	104
35. Hood	106
36. Falling	108
37. Rose	110
38. Boom	113
39. Blocks	115
40. Loss	117
41. Seeds	120
42. Lunch	122
43. Detection	124
44. Cake	126
45. Kool-Aid	128
46. Tacos	131
47. Rain	133
48. Hiking	135

49. Giving Tree	137
50. Impossible	139
51. Oh Crap	141
52. Diary	144
Part Three	146
The Voice and Silence of Our Attention	147
Pay Attention	150
The Antidote	152
Acknowledgments	156
Influences	158
Endnotes	160

"I would much rather have men ask why I have no statue, than why I have one."
> ~ Cato the Elder, Roman Statesman and Philosopher

"Failure is simply an unsatisfactory solution which someone has accepted as one's final solution."
> ~ Michael Weber, Professional Wonder-Worker

Letter to the Reader

Dear Reader,

Life is hard. Not equally hard for all of us, but everyone we encounter faces challenges. Of course, life gets simpler when we let autopilot take over. But simpler is not better, nor is it easier.

The worst, and scariest, feature of autopilot is not noticing when it engages. For me, when autopilot kicks in, I commonly find myself wanting *things* I don't care about because I believe they will bring me the joy that I am missing in that moment. But, *things* rarely do. *Arriving at my destination* or *having the thing* provides only a moment of happiness. These are sometimes physical things that I feel have, or will give me, status like clothing, types of vehicles, or new technology. Sometimes they are indicators of completing something like an award, certificate, or degree. They may also be achievements, such as a specific vacation, a title at work, or writing a book. Even having friends or children, the joy isn't in *having them*, but in sharing time and experiences. Genuine joy is found in the effort or work it takes to get to where I want to be and to achieve what I want to achieve.

It's not just *things* that let me down. I waste time in my head trying to revisit past events. Sometimes, I am hoping to reclaim the good ones. Or I am trying to forget all the awkward and uncomfortable moments by rehashing a conversation in a thousand different ways. It isn't just the past. I also spend too much time attempting to invoke my will on the future.

These claims, the ones that sound like, *I'll be happy when I get this thing,* or, *I'll be able to coast after this accomplishment,* do not represent my honest experience. Like most people, these false claims of *peak happiness* continue to leave me wanting. Left unsatisfied, I chase after more.

> "The end never justifies the means because there is no end; there are only means."
>
> ~ Penn Jillette, Entertainer

It's taken me nearly forty years to come to this point. I struggled to differentiate whether advice was good or bad for me, sometimes rejecting the good advice or accepting the bad. I felt like I was too far from who I was supposed to be. I struggled to fit in or to feel like I belonged anywhere. I was often told, or just pressured, to become something that didn't feel right.

The first discovery that introduced more intentionality into my life was that I didn't need to change to be sufficient. The second discovery was that I was not stuck being who I was. I am capable of growth. The third discovery was that the journey far outweighs the destination.

In this book, I will share the stories and events that have taught me the most valuable life lessons. I will point you toward the creators and influences that shaped my journey and share how they have entered my life.

In March 2020, my company sent everyone to work from home for "the next three weeks" to stem the spread of COVID-19. My team did a great job keeping the work-stuff moving forward. On the first Friday, I knew I needed to check in on the well-being of everyone. The mood was heavy around the world. I shared an update about me and my family, shared some resources that might lighten their loads, and then told a few jokes. I closed with a request to check in and let me know how they were doing. I received overwhelmingly positive feedback from my team and have since sent a note almost every Friday. The weekly notes have allowed me to put into words the many things I have learned throughout my life. Those check-ins are the basis of the articles in this book.

In my journey, I have discovered the value of being considerate about how I go through life. I am happiest when I pay attention—when I am aware of my thoughts and feelings and how they impact the people and the world around me. I experience the most joy when I support and serve those around me.

Take care,

Richard | hello@RichardIngram.me
Be curious, be kind, be whole, do good things.

INTRODUCTION

Perspective. Evelyn Ingram (age 11), artist.

I get so excited by a good book that I want to rush through it. Going fast, I miss out on or forget critical ideas. I don't take the time to stop and consider an idea. I miss out on discovering many new ways to apply what I am learning to my life. I designed this book for people like me to slow down. My recommendation is to read one entry per week for a year. But I also suffer from the affliction of rejecting authority. So, read however many you want.

If you opt to follow my advice, assume each topic applies directly to you. Your mission is to determine how to apply my story, and the stories and lessons from others that have inspired me along the way, to your circumstances.

Be creative and be open. The less a subject seems relevant to you, the harder you should try to prove that impulse wrong. Consider discussing the topic with those in your life. Each week, intentionally apply the ideas. Check in to see how it went. Be honest with yourself if it doesn't go well.

> "Life is what happens to you while you're busy making other plans."
> ~ John Lennon | "Beautiful Boy (Darling Boy)"

My goal is to live a full life where I experience the rich texture, no matter the circumstances. Growth is a lifelong mission. Make progress every chance you get, but not at the expense of living life.

Part One

Consider this first section foundational. Over many years, I have collected wisdom from those before me. The following are the most practical for me and establish an understanding of myself and others.

Values

> "Small suggestion: don't make 'being young' part of your identity. It'll get harder to feel like yourself with each passing year..."
>
> ~ @BatKaren | Twitter post

Going through life, we gather and collect ideas. We paste these ideas into a mental scrapbook that inevitably influences or overtakes our thoughts. We fill our pages with things we've intentionally selected—a desired school, career, or mate. We fill other pages unintentionally with ideas from our relatives, neighbors, and the media we consume. We clip out scraps and pieces from books, movies, family, the people we see, or unknowingly from other sources. Some pages are just filled with idealized thinking.

I tried to go to college right after high school. It wasn't a good fit for me at the time. I felt like a failure when I quit. I convinced myself that I was inferior to everyone else. I grew to hate social events. High school and college football are a huge deal in Texas. So, if the topic of football came up, I knew it was just a matter of time until people started talking about colleges. "Where did you go to school?" The question itself so clearly pointed out I was *supposed* to already have a degree.

These scrapbook pages serve as a guide to measure our desires, intentions, hopes, and dreams. We measure the success of our days against what we think life should be for us. If we aren't paying attention, the guideposts we set for what we most value won't even be things we truly care about, rather, things that we feel we are supposed to care about. When we inspect what we hold close and find that those beliefs haven't grown with us, it is time to consider pruning.

My scrapbook contains a page that, as I have grown older and taken on new life experiences, has shifted throughout the years, titled *Values*. Currently, this page in my scrapbook includes five key sections:

1. Do I Matter To You (DIMTY)
2. What Matters Most (WMM)
3. Understanding
4. Compassion
5. Be curious, be kind, be whole, do good things.

DIMTY

This first section highlights the question DIMTY—*Do I Matter To You?* My friend Andy Hickman is a professional speaker and magician. In Andy's book *Stuff That Really Matters,* he explains that his acronym 'DIMTY' represents a question we often silently ask ourselves when facing someone who seems to be focused on anything other than our interaction: DIMTY.

There is a deep psychological need to belong and to be valued. Our brains are still configured for life in the tribal plains. We fear being rejected due to our evolutionary response to preserve our role in the tribe. Life outside the tribe meant death. Nearly every interaction starts with the question, even if only as an undetected, subconscious feeling—do I matter to you?

A server at a restaurant didn't listen to your order. The distracted receptionist didn't instruct you clearly. The person you were sharing a personal story with began typing on their phone. If you have experienced any of these situations, then you know what it feels like when someone answers your DIMTY with *No.* Whether intentionally or unintentionally, they are telling you that, in that moment, you don't matter. We want to matter. We need to matter. We can change so much by answering *Yes* to the silent question running through someone's head when they encounter you: DIMTY?

WMM

Michael Weber, a Wonder-Worker and public speaker, said in a live lecture that when we need to focus, we should ask, *What Matters Most?* When we have that answer, we can prioritize properly and focus on what matters most.

Time and other resources spent in any one area take away from spending that time in other areas. When we focus on our career, family, or hobbies, time is taken away from something else. Understanding those trade-offs is key to successfully prioritizing WMM so that we can allocate our time in the way that leads us to the experiences that are most fulfilling in our lives. If we are constantly tackling what is directly in front of us at any given moment, we can easily miss the things that are truly important to our lives.

Once we clearly understand what matters most to ourselves, we can then, carefully and openly, listen to and ask questions of others. We can help them identify WMM to them. When our WMMs intersect, we can intentionally collaborate and move each other closer to our respective targets.

One of the biggest traps that we must avoid when deciding where to spend our time is the phenomenon known as a "fear of missing out" or FOMO. Advertisers have learned to manipulate this fear to sell more products. They pepper us with an act now or a limited-time offer, which creates a fear of being left behind. And we all have people in our lives who apply the same tactics when trying to re-prioritize where we spend our time. They say that if you don't go to this concert or join them for those drinks, you'll be missing out on something special. Without fully understanding what matters most to you and prioritizing your time accordingly, you easily fall into the FOMO trap. When we make time for the wrong things, we miss out on those that are truly special.

Oliver Burkeman, the author of *Four Thousand Weeks: Time Management for Mortals*, suggests that we pivot FOMO into JOMO or the Joy of Missing Out. The fear of missing out on something is an irrational fear. It is irrational because we are constantly and inevitably missing out on something. It is an unavoidable situation. Instead, we should determine what matters most right now and invest (not spend) our time and energy in those things. We will find joy in that worthy investment into our rest, play, or work. Don't pay attention; invest attention.

UNDERSTANDING AND COMPASSION

We should not only *accept* who we are, but we should also be *comfortable* with ourselves. I want to create an environment that encourages others to be fully who they are. In return, I need to be comfortable being myself. Step one is knowing who I am.

In *Dare to Lead*, author Brené Brown recommends selecting two key core values. She says direct and explicit values will allow us to make decisions more easily. We will be stronger leaders and followers, especially during times of adversity. In *The Subtle Art of Not Giving a F*ck*, author Mark Manson suggests values should be both immediate and controllable. For example, I shouldn't tie a core value to being young, since I cannot control growing older. I combined these authors' suggestions and identified two core, controllable values that I prioritize as central to my being.

1. *Understanding* means to "stand in the midst of." It is not enough to know or see each other; we must be *in it* to truly understand each other.

2. *Compassion* means "to suffer together." Empathy is a powerful ability for connecting, but acting on empathy is deeply altering for everyone involved. We cannot touch without being touched.

BE CURIOUS, BE KIND, BE WHOLE, DO GOOD THINGS.

Understanding and compassion are active values. These are forms of *doing*, which have been critical to all the success I have experienced. Over time, I have found four themes that continue to weave through most of what I believe: *Be curious, be kind, be whole, do good things.*

This simplified core philosophy reminds me how I can simultaneously accept who I currently am and still strive toward progress. The focus on *being* and *doing* has dramatically benefited how I view life, and, in turn, improved my appreciation and quality of life. They serve as a reminder to find balance and focus on what is important to me. Trying to jump into a massive change that ultimately fails has never worked for me. Consistency has led to greater change over time.

Be Curious ~ My curiosity means I know a bit about many things. Being inquisitive and having a basic understanding of a wide range of topics has led me to understand new concepts faster. It has enhanced my creativity when problem-solving and allowed me to connect with people more easily.

Everything we know and learn goes into our bag of tricks for later use. Curiosity enables us to develop tools, skills, and solutions before we need them. Our curiosity lets us learn more about those around us, expanding our ability to understand, empathize, and influence each other.

Be Kind ~ I feel better and less stressed when I am kind. I know others recognize and can feel it as well. When I assume the best intentions in others, I am right most of the time. Mistakes are rare.

We make the best decisions we can based on our life experiences at that point. When there is safety in allowing for error and differences, we can develop trust. This level of comfort allows everyone to be themselves—their entire selves—and leaves room for others to contribute their perspective and ideas, giving you access to points of view you wouldn't have in an environment of fear and mistrust.

Be Whole ~ I am most comfortable when I accept who I am and allow myself to be complete. I connect more fully when I create a safe space for other people to be themselves.

Outside of where we are most comfortable, we put up a guard as a safety buffer. This armor causes us to protect ourselves by holding back, thus creating a small level of dishonesty. While the dishonesty may be imperceptible, it creates a layer of distrust. Trust, especially vulnerability-based trust, is critical to building the best relationship possible. When we bring out the entirety of who we are and allow ourselves to be wholly ourselves, unexpected results come from it.

Do Good Things ~ This one is far more loaded. I feel greater satisfaction when I am actively *doing*. This is especially true when my *doing* yields good things.

Michael Weber exposed me to the perspective of *doing* versus *being*. He said the idea originated with R. Buckminster Fuller's book *I Seem to Be a Verb*. Weber discusses on the podcast *Jesse's Office*[1] that he is "better and happier in a verb mindset than as a noun mindset." A verb mindset is "not a label of person, place, or thing—those have borders, whereas actions are not constrained." He said that doing, which he called a "verb state," is far better than any "noun state" or labels that we've assigned to ourselves. We easily fall short of a label or description because we don't meet the ideal image attached to that label. When we tie our identity to *being* something, it can be very difficult to know if or when we arrive. A goal of *doing* is far more attainable and satisfying. With that accomplishment, we are moving forward in our lives and becoming more fulfilled. If we are doing things, they might as well be good things. The vagueness of the *things* is intentional—planning is essential, but without *doing,* the planning is futile.

Ultimately, the scrapbook page in my mind titled "Values" boils down to these two concepts: pay attention and be intentional. To let someone know they matter to me, I must invest attention in them and intentionally address their needs. To know what matters most to me, I must pay attention to my needs and intentionally address them. For me to understand, I must pay attention. To have compassion, I must act intentionally. The mission becomes *pay attention* and *be intentional*, or…

> Be curious, be kind, be whole, do good things.

MINDSET

There are many more scrapbook pages in my mind, and in the pages to follow, I will share some of the greatest hits—the experiences, movies I watched, books I read, and lessons I learned that have shaped who I am, who I want to be, and where I want to go. I hope that this book can help you as you wrestle with some of the same questions in your own life. If nothing else, there are some great stories in the mix.

I believed for a long time that I was just *who I was*. I felt stuck. Carol Dweck is a psychologist, researcher, and the author of *Mindset: The New Psychology of Success*. In her book, she explains the two primary modes of thinking: 1. Fixed, and 2. Growth. Our environment and upbringing condition us to believe one of two things: that our personal qualities, such as intelligence and empathy, are innate, unchangeable, and fixed, or that those qualities are capable of changing and guiding us to growth. This is similar to the belief that we are born a certain way (nature) or raised a certain way (nurture). The answer is the same as the nature versus nurture debate: **both** are factors.

However, mindset is a choice. If you believe you are stuck, fixed in your capabilities, then you are right. If you believe you can grow and change, you are right. *Choose your own adventure.*

Blind Men and the Elephant

The poem below, written by John Godfrey Saxe (1872), is based on an ancient Hindu fable. Over the years, I have used this poem as a tool to describe the personal limitations of understanding because of perspective, bias, and arrogance. Most often, I am one of the blind men, though sometimes I am the misunderstood elephant.

THE BLIND MEN AND THE ELEPHANT.[2]
A HINDOO FABLE.

I.

IT was six men of Indostan
To learning much inclined,
Who went to see the Elephant
(Though all of them were blind),
That each by observation
Might satisfy his mind.

II.

The *First* approached the Elephant,
And happening to fall
Against his broad and sturdy side,
At once began to bawl:
"God bless me!—but the Elephant
Is very like a wall!"

III.

The *Second*, feeling of the tusk,
Cried: "Ho!—what have we here

So very round and smooth and sharp?
To me 't is mighty clear
This wonder of an Elephant
Is very like a spear!"

IV.
The *Third* approached the animal,
And happening to take
The squirming trunk within his hands,
Thus boldly up and spake:
"I see," quoth he, "the Elephant
Is very like a snake!"

V.
The *Fourth* reached out his eager hand,
And felt about the knee.
"What most this wondrous beast is like
Is mighty plain," quoth he;
"'Tis clear enough the Elephant
Is very like a tree!"

VI.
The *Fifth*, who chanced to touch the

ear,
Said: "E'en the blindest man
Can tell what this resembles most;
Deny the fact who can,
This marvel of an Elephant
Is very like a fan!"

VII.
The *Sixth* no sooner had begun
About the beast to grope,
Than, seizing on the swinging tail
That fell within his scope,
"I see," quoth he, "the Elephant
Is very like a rope!"

VIII.
And so these men of Indostan
Disputed loud and long,
Each in his own opinion
Exceeding stiff and strong,
Though each was partly in the right,
And all were in the wrong!

MORAL.
So, oft in theologic wars

The disputants, I ween,
Rail on in utter ignorance
Of what each other mean,
And prate about an Elephant
Not one of them has seen!

PETS OF THE MIND

Sometimes I glimpse myself in a mirror, and I am surprised. Without a mirror or photos, I can't see myself. I spend most of my time looking at other people, yet, when I look in the mirror, I'm able to recognize the person I see as me. Much like hearing a recording of my voice, I don't look or sound the way I think I do. Sometimes I am thinner or heavier than I thought. I may look better, or worse, or, *oh my gosh a pimple!* The way I look at any given moment depends on angles, lighting, my mood then or now, the setting, and many other factors.

The image in the mirror isn't actually me; it is a piece of glass with reflective material. A photograph isn't me either; it is a piece of paper with ink. Like the blind men, my perspective is limited to the internal and external environmental factors and influences of that moment in time. Generously sharing my ideas, thoughts, and feelings and encouraging others to do the same helps me to have a more complete picture of my life. With a better understanding of my thinking machine, I can see myself and others more clearly.

Before I can share my process with you, I need to share the theory behind the system. Dr. Rick Hanson put together a formula for explaining why we do what we do. Our brain has three primary parts, with each part having a unique purpose:

- The first area is the **lizard** brain, or reptile brain, which is the brain stem. This manages our most basic systems like breathing, our heart beating, and making immediate decisions—to avoid being eaten. This is also the part of the brain that generates our anxiety.[3]

- The second is our **mouse** brain, or mammal brain, which is the limbic system, and it addresses our emotions and desires. These are not as automatic as the lizard brain's fight, flight, or freeze response. They are still about maintaining life, but also seeking rewards and avoiding penalties.[4]

- The third area of our brain is the **monkey** brain, or primate brain, which is the cortex. The cortex is the center for all higher functions. This part of our brain makes our mental maps of the world and drives our desire for connectedness with others.[5]

The lizard brain, or brain stem, manages our basic life-saving functions. Our mouse brain, or limbic system, manages our emotions and desires. The monkey brain, or cortex, is the center of all higher functions and the desire for connection. These segments are real, distinct, and biologically identifiable areas of the brain. I am more capable of managing my emotions and reactions when I better understand the functions of each area.

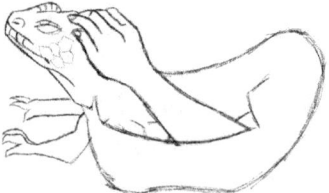

Pet the Lizard. Evelyn Ingram (age 11), artist.

Petting the lizard is acknowledging how we experience feelings such as anxiety. Our lizard brain is trying to keep us safe from harm. Most of the time, I am not at risk, so my lizard might get twitchy and respond to situations that aren't dangerous for me. Have you ever seen a fuzz ball on the ground and thought it was a critter? Before you can process what is happening, it fills your body with adrenaline; you might even yell out. This is the lizard brain reacting to a non-existent danger. We are safe the entire time despite the chemical response.

To pet the lizard is taking deep breaths, then relaxing the muscles throughout the body. It is accepting all of our emotions at face value, whether they are good or bad. If we can remind our lizard when we are safe, it becomes easier to accept and process our responses to fear so that we don't become overrun with stress or act irrationally.

Feed the Mouse. E. Ingram, artist.

Feeding the mouse is having gratitude. It may be as simple as acknowledging the basics of life, food, air, and gainful employment. The recognition and appreciation for the beauty of life helps to feed our mouse. Paying close attention to ourselves and those near us will uncover things to be grateful for.

Hug the Monkey. E. Ingram, artist.

Hugging the monkey centers on care. This comes into play when we recall someone who cares for us, someone we care for, or just a sense of belonging.

As humans, we use our five senses to process our experiences through our brains. Because of their physical placement, these systems always process in the same order—lizard, mouse, monkey. Every experience we have goes from lizard, maybe to mouse, then maybe to monkey. So, each experience must traverse each of the various creatures to get to deep thinking. Since these reactions and responses are critical to our survival, we cannot ignore them. But when we care for and feed our creatures, they settle. When our pets settle, we are happier, more focused, and more productive.

> "Everyone is screwed up, broken, clingy and scared, even the people who seem to have it most together. They are much more like you than you would believe, so try not to compare your insides to other people's outsides."[6]
>
> ~ Anne Lamott

I find comfort in studying psychology. I sometimes feel isolated when I am experiencing big emotions. The isolation makes me feel broken—as though I am not as prepared for life as those around me. As I have discovered that others have similar experiences, I have become more patient with myself as I grow.

System 1 and System 2

Dr. Hanson's theory isn't the only theory that has influenced how I think. Psychologists and other researchers have tried to classify our decision-making patterns in a variety of ways over the years. These categories are artificial constructs that help us more clearly understand how our brain makes choices so we can categorize and improve the way we process and act on our thoughts. Daniel Kahneman describes one of these two-part models in great detail in his book *Thinking, Fast and Slow*. He has created a two-system model to explain how the speed with which we process thoughts affects our reactions:

- System 1 is quick, instinctive, and functions automatically with almost no exerted effort and no sense of voluntary control.

- System 2 takes more care and attention to decision-making. This is when we employ any subjective experience like concentrating, choosing, or agency to process the complex problems we face.

We want to believe we use System 2 most of the time, but we don't. Our brains are lazy, and they will defer to System 1 every chance they get. System 1 is so fast that it is very confident and convincing. It makes patterns, assumptions, and develops shortcuts for the quickest response. System 2 is very supportive of System 1 because it's easy to use those shortcuts as assumptions for facts and turn them into beliefs.

When my kids see new food, they reject it instantly. The unfamiliar color, smell, or texture are cues to System 1 to avoid it. After some coaxing, maybe a little bribery, I can get them to try it. Most often when they assume they won't like something—they don't. If I can get them to think they might like it—they usually do. Either way, convincing them to follow System 2 thinking to make an honest attempt lets them learn if they like it.

In the same vein, I try to avoid bias and prejudice in my decision-making by pausing to push my lazy System 2 thinking into action. When I find myself in a rut of being sleepy, grumpy, angry, or sad, I spend some time trying to find the reason. More often than not, System 1 is saying, "You are annoyed," or, "You are tired," and really, I am not. But System 2's trusting nature believes those messages to be true until I stir the system to wake up and issue the care and attention it needs to assess a situation properly. Do I give new things a fair shake? Are old memories skewing new experiences? Am I being present or turning all decisions over to System 1?

When considering the analogy of the elephant, we see how easily what we *know* can be flawed. One of my favorite moments in a movie is from *Men in Black*. If you haven't seen it, you should. It is about a police officer who is invited to work for a secret government agency that handles aliens. Tommy Lee Jones's character Agent K is sitting on a bench trying to recruit an NYPD officer played by Will Smith (aka the Fresh Prince of Bel-Air). Agent K says, "Fifteen hundred years ago, everybody knew the Earth was the center of the universe. Five hundred years ago, everybody knew the Earth was flat. And fifteen minutes ago, you knew that people were alone on this planet. Imagine what you'll know tomorrow."

Things we know to be real, many of which may even be our shared understanding, might still be inaccurate. We regularly make mistakes when thinking. As we better understand these errors, called fallacies, we can identify when those situations arise. We can then pause, engage System 2 thinking, and reflect before proceeding.

One of these fallacies is the fragility and weakness of our memories. Even strong and vivid memories are often filled with inaccuracies. Current research in wrongful convictions shows that almost seventy percent of overturned cases were based on eyewitness testimony.[7]

Our brains, on average, have about 70,000 thoughts per day. Besides these thoughts muddying the water, System 1 is constantly telling System 2, *Been there, done that*. This is a heuristic, which is essentially a thinking shortcut. This shortcut is forcing us to guess what will happen based on assumptions from our experiences. We trust ourselves, our experiences, and our perception of what is happening more than the data that exists.

Availability Bias

There is a tendency called availability bias that rules our assumptions by applying faulty or limited memories of a situation.[8] This bias sneaks up on us when we use our recollection of examples to determine how often those things actually occur. Shark attacks are a common reason people won't swim in the ocean. When you look at the data, there are about eight annual deaths per year across the entire world. With that data, you should be far more afraid of driving to the beach instead of being in the water. I'm intentionally not sharing the vehicle deaths, but it is over sixty times higher than sharks, airplanes, and tornados combined.[9] [10] [11] [12]

In smaller ways, availability bias has influenced how I feel about someone. This feeling can go both ways. Either a couple of great experiences or a couple of terrible interactions can influence how I feel about every interaction with them. It impacts how I feel about work or specific tasks, and how I feel about brands. It affects my mood and interactions. Using limited, but vivid, memories, I make assumptions about what to expect in an upcoming encounter and alter my mood and approach before anything occurs.

Human instincts have been fine-tuned throughout history, evolving over a very long time. These instincts have developed for a reason, and in situations of high risk, we should trust them. When a tiger is charging, I immediately know danger based on the orange and black fur, sharp teeth, giant paws, and wild eyes, so I run. If I had to take the time to catalog the event and evaluate the situation before acting, I would be dead. The same can't be said for all biases. When we have time, we shouldn't make major decisions based on gut alone. We should take a minute to look at the information at hand and evaluate the data.

Am I starting an interaction fresh or assuming frustration or annoyance? Do I have evidence that this time will be the same? Can I justify how I am feeling this time? Am I stirring System 2 enough so it will engage and process this situation? Have I petted the lizard, fed the mouse, and hugged the monkey?

Be curious, be kind, be whole, do good things.

Part Two

The following fifty two essays were intended to be read one per week. However, I wholeheartedly encourage rebellion. So do whatever you want.

One

Walter

Used with permission.

I've had many jobs. I worked for family members at a gun store and as an HVAC technician. I was a cart boy at a golf course, a car mechanic, supported an insurance agency, built websites, and others I am certainly forgetting. While the most interesting job I've ever had was working in my parents' magic store, the most influential was working as an agent taking calls at a call center. I was only there for eighteen months but got at least eighteen years of life lessons. One of my craziest calls was a person calling maintenance because their building was on fire. I asked if 911 was already notified and they weren't. I said, "Please hang up, head outside immediately, and then call 911."

I'd joke the call center had one of each personality, culture, economic situation, race, and in many cases, a variety of disorders. I learned to connect and integrate with people who had a variety of life experiences. I made lifelong friends and have carried those lessons with me since.

One such friend was Walter. He was the client on the contract I supported. He was far less intimidating than some of the other "suits" that loitered. He was also key in my transition to the company I am still at twenty years later. We became fast friends and remained close until his passing. He was kind, patient, and listened with intensity. One day in the break room, the news was reporting *civil unrest* in response to racism. I said to Walter, "I'm pretty sure we are one generation away from racism disappearing. My kids don't understand the idea of racism."

Walter paused, then simultaneously kindly and firmly said, "I hope so, because my boys understand it too well." He told me his story. Growing up his was the only black family in his Wisconsin neighborhood. He told me about his struggle to teach his kids to be kind and patient in a world that was tilted against them. As he shared his story, I thought about my experiences. I felt like I had *earned* everything. I recalled all the referrals, recommendations, and free passes. I remembered some of the crazy things I'd done and gotten away with just a warning.

Privilege isn't getting away with something instead of getting caught. Privilege is getting away with stuff after being caught. Privilege is blind to itself, both giving and getting it. The first abuse of power is not realizing that I have it. It is difficult to differentiate what was my *hard work*, versus what

I achieved within a supportive environment and network that eased my path. I learned from Walter that we must hear other people's stories. He showed me that sharing my privilege does nothing to diminish it.

Have I heard your story? Do you know mine? Am I generous in sharing my privilege?

Be curious, be kind, be whole, do good things.

Two

Labels

Photo credit: Jack Shalom
JackShalom.net

"Her name was Magill, and she called herself Lil, but everyone knew her as Nancy."

~ The Beatles | "Rocky Raccoon"

In and Of Itself is a documentary of a theatrical magic show by Derek DelGaudio. As guests arrived at the Broadway theater, they chose a card from a wall. Each card had "I AM" followed by an identity such as blogger, writer, nobody, or daughter. No further instructions were provided.

During the show, Derek told a version of *The Blind Men and The Elephant*. Then he highlighted the constraining nature of the blind men's labeling. He suggested perhaps the elephant wasn't an elephant at all. The blind men could have been wrong about what they were touching. But just by labeling this creature as an *elephant,* that is what it became.

Labels can be very difficult to apply. There is not always a label that fits perfectly, so we stretch and torture them. We crave labels, wanting to attach them to everything. Including ourselves and others. We let others label us, and they let us label them. Once we've got a label in place, we let what we already know about other things with the same label fill the gaps without even realizing it. We let those labels define our essence. They start to define our worth, painting a picture of our successes or failures. This is the limiting nature of labels.

Labels are like a cheap, ill-fitting sweater: itchy, confining, and uncomfortable. They don't fit because of the finite nature of their description—the essence of a noun. We use these labels to stereotype—to guess or presume information we don't have. I won't spoil the ending of Derek's show, but know that people deeply want to be seen. Sometimes for who they are, sometimes for who they want to be.

Labels are a shortcut. The problem with shortcuts is they take you where the shortcut leads and not where the real path goes. The map I've drawn for my life is filled with shortcuts. It doesn't consider who I am and where I need to be. I often don't know what I need until I have found it. In our own way, we get in our own way.

In Michael Weber's doing versus being mindset discussed earlier, he said he is "a better person that is much happier when in a verb mindset instead of a noun mindset." Since nouns describe a person, place, or thing, they have borders, limits that can be immutable. Conversely, a verb is defined by its *doing*. The verb state is preferred because it is not about what I am, but what I do. It is easier to give up when we don't live up to our label, and labels can't even accurately identify who we are. If we really want to change, we must get into the verb mindset.

We decide to make things, help people, create, build, etc. We can find the verb things we can accomplish and get out of the noun loop. If you want to be more, do more. If you want something you've never had, you've got to do something you've never done.

Am I being me or what my label says I should be? Can I shed my label? Can I remove the sticky residue left behind? How can I avoid constraining others?

Be curious, be kind, be whole, do good things.

Three

Curiosity

Inspector Clouseau: Does your dog bite?
Hotel Clerk: No.
Clouseau: Nice doggie. [Dog barks and bites Clouseau] I thought you said your dog did not bite!
Clerk: That is not my dog.
The Pink Panther Strikes Again (1976)

Asking questions and being curious are powerful habits worth nurturing. When exploring new thoughts and ideas, it's difficult to know what questions to ask. Often, the first question is the least important. Listening to the answer and continuing to explore is where the real discovery occurs.

Simon Sinek is the author of *Start with Why*, a book that highlights the importance of understanding why we are doing things. In his TED Talk, he shares an exercise useful for digging past the surface-level reasons. He says that, to dig deep enough to understand our purpose, we should continue to ask *Why?* five times.[13]

We can apply the 5-why rule when we seek to understand ourselves and our motivations. When setting a personal goal, I try to dig five levels into why I want to accomplish it. When the going inevitably gets tough, I think back to those answers, reflect on my purpose, and persevere.

I set a personal goal to become fluent in Spanish. I had many small reasons. I initially told myself that the reason I wanted to learn Spanish was to be able to speak to my friends who are already fluent. However, after using the 5-whys to explore my motivation, my reasons turned out to be much deeper. I discovered that if I learned to think in a second language, I would become a more effective communicator in my native language. The more robustly I understand words, the more clarity I can have in my usage.

I am five hundred days into learning Spanish. While I am learning a lot, I am still not to the stage of being fluent, nor thinking in Spanish. Knowing that this is my ultimate goal, I find that taking a lesson every day is easier.

Where can I be more inquisitive? When should I ask follow-up questions? Do I deeply understand the *why* behind my goals? When helping others, can we work together to find the question they wanted to ask?

Be curious, be kind, be whole, do good things.

Four

Coins

"I hate working from home."

~ Stephanie (age 32), Firefighter

Have you ever experienced something, and it just hits you differently than it did before? Something you thought you understood well gets a new light shone on it, and it takes on new meaning.

In the movie *Throw Mama from the Train*, Owen (Danny DeVito) is a naïve aspiring writer who takes a writing class from Larry (Billy Crystal). Owen obsessively badgers Larry for feedback on his story. Through their conversations, Owen, who hates his mother, learns that Larry hates his ex-wife. After much pestering, Larry finally gives Owen feedback on his story. He tells him that the story lacks motivation. Larry recommends Owen watch Hitchcock's famous *Strangers on a Train* for inspiration. As Owen watches the movie, he mistakes Larry's advice as a secret message. He is now inspired and tries to convince Larry to kill Owen's mother. In exchange, Owen would kill Larry's ex-wife.

As they continue to spend time together, Owen shares that he has a coin collection. In one scene he begs Larry to look at his coin collection. Owen pulls out his coins, and Larry immediately sees they are just modern, average-looking nickels and dimes. "The purpose of a coin collection is that the coins are worth something, Owen," said Larry.

Owen replies, "Oh, but they are. This one here I got in change... when my dad took me to see Peter, Paul, and Mary. And this one I got in change when I bought a hot dog at the circus. My daddy let me keep the change. He always let me keep the change."

Owen didn't collect the coins for their face value, age, or rarity. Yet, they were of immeasurable worth to Owen. Everything I see is from *my* perspective. My own life and experiences influence my perspective. It will always be my default.

I have been Owen—sharing something I care deeply about, just to have it dismissed by someone that didn't understand. I have been Larry—not understanding someone's passion and dismissing it as misguided. Now, whenever someone presents me with something they are excited about, I try to understand the excitement from their perspective. If the object of their passion seems mundane, I know I need to really dig in. I try to see what brings them joy from their eyes.

When I am presented with others' *coin collections*, can I step away from my default so I can see the true value? Am I open to another point of view? Have I seen your coin collection? Can I show you mine?

Be curious, be kind, be whole, do good things.

Five

Seeing

Ethan is the youngest in our family. His sister is about eight minutes older. He's exceptionally quiet, and, unfortunately for him, has my twisted sense of humor. Ethan tagged along with his oldest brother, Chase, for a trip to the optometrist. Chase was in the chair, going through the eye chart.

Ethan sat to the side with Mom, started giggling, then full-body laughing. When Mom asked what was going on, he said, "He's getting them *all* wrong!" Immediately interested, the doctor had them trade places. She asked Ethan to identify the letters on the wall across the room. After the first couple of lines, he missed nearly every one of them. It turned out that

Ethan was the one getting the letters wrong. His eyesight was so poor that he also needed corrective lenses.

Sometimes I have to remind myself that *I* may be the one who needs glasses. I fall prey to System 1 thinking and easily identify the shortcomings in others to quickly determine how other people *should be*.

Where do I not see clearly and assume it is you? Am I casting stones from my glass house? Will I be open to considering I am the problem?

Be curious, be kind, be whole, do good things.

Six

Unfinished

In 2017, the highly destructive Hurricane Harvey hit Texas and Louisiana. This storm may have slowed after landfall, but it hovered, dropping heavy rain for four days, resulting in flooding and a tremendous amount of damage. The Red Cross, community groups, and churches across the United States organized crews of volunteers to clean up and support those affected. In training as a Red Cross volunteer, I learned that families only get access to insurance money after the adjuster has visited the site. Unfortunately, insurance adjusters will not assess damage until the space is clear and cleaned out.

We left Prosper, Texas at 4:00 a.m. on Saturday. I hauled a trailer full of demolition tools and a carload of neighbors down to the Houston area (a four-hour drive). The Red Cross gave us four addresses to tend to over the next two days. If you've ever cleaned up after flooding or storms, you know it is hard and dirty work. The houses were without power, and water had been standing within the house for about two weeks. Without too vivid of a picture, the smells and rot were overwhelming. Emotions were high as families had lost family members, homes, and heirlooms. On top of it all, they dealt with looters every night.

We finished two of the houses on the first day, and that night we went to an assigned area high school. We ate PB&J sandwiches, showered in the locker room, and slept on the gymnasium floor. The next day, we headed off to work on the last two houses assigned to our crew. We were not able to finish the work.

I went back years later, and Houston was still recovering from the damage that the storm left behind. The work was hard, and the days were long, seeming to be never-ending. We filled shovel after shovel of stomach-turning sludge and cut out soggy, rotted sections of drywall. There was muscle fatigue from hauling waterlogged, extra heavy furniture.

Those days were exceptionally sad, but it was also one of the most rewarding and fulfilling experiences of my life. I left there with a new appreciation for the good fortune in my life. We felt the family's joy when our crew showed up to help them. Tears flowed when we *discovered* something the owner cared about. I bonded with people I would otherwise never have met. I connected with my neighbors that went with me, and we shared the burden of the labor.

Sometimes work can be unfulfilling, especially if it is long, dirty, or hard work. However, when I connect with those I work with, I see the value of what I am doing through the eyes of those I am serving. We celebrate the small wins along the way, and we can experience the rich and fulfilling joy of the effort. We can find beauty in the mundane.

Do I connect with those working with me? Am I appreciating my contribution to our mission? Have I recognized and celebrated the steps along the way?

Be curious, be kind, be whole, do good things.

Seven

Fooling

"The first principle is that you must not fool yourself, and you are the easiest person to fool."

~Richard Feynman, Physicist

Growing up in a magic store, I spent a disturbing amount of time practicing secret moves over and over. Young magicians make the mistake of watching their hands while practicing. This can lead to issues when performing, as it will look very different from their point of view than to the spectator. To fix this, a magician will practice in front of a mirror.

I had been practicing one trick in particular for days and, once I simulated the audience's perspective, I had finally *perfected* the trickery. After reaching this peak of perfection, I was stoked to show off my miracle. I performed it for my dad, who suggested it looked good. Then he gave me a lot of feedback. In fact, it was too much feedback for something that "looked good."

I tried to hear him but, I already knew—after watching myself perform the trick in the mirror—it indeed was magic. In a great dispute with my father, who, at the time, I knew must be blind, we video-taped my performance. This was a far bigger ordeal back before smart phones, but I was glad to record evidence of my magical powers so he could see my trick was genius. The first time through was hideous. It did not look good. In fact, it was terrible. What had happened? Why was this so different from what I was doing before?

I watched the video several times before I noticed my eyes. Each time I did the *funny business*, I would blink. It was quick. But in slow motion, I'd seen my mistake. The setup would be fine, then my eyes closed during the magical state–which was not so magical to those with their eyes open.

This is a lesson I continue to learn. It is hard to know where I honestly stand. I overestimate my abilities. I underestimate my abilities. Taking different perspectives than my own and really listening to others can help me calibrate. Once I have a clear picture of where I am, I can grow.

Am I blinking at my shortcomings so I can't see them? Where can I use mirrors, video, or those caring individuals around me to see where I really am? Can I offer better advice? Can I be more open to feedback?

Be curious, be kind, be whole, do good things.

Eight

The Letter

Jeff was my best friend growing up. His mom was my second mom. We were born a week apart in the same hospital. We did everything together. In fourth grade, his dad's company relocated their family to Phoenix. My world fell apart. I needed him. He filled in where I fell short. Our parents let us spend the summer together alternating states each year. Typical of teenagers, our lives grew apart. But we stay in touch to this day, picking up right where we left off.

I was fifteen years old when I tagged along to his summer camp in Arizona. Towards the end of the week, our camp counselor had us write a letter to ourselves. He specifically suggested we give ourselves advice, share what's going well, and anything that was bothering us. I wasn't much of a feeling-sharer, but I tightly sealed my deepest fifteen-year-old-kid's feelings in this letter. We self-addressed, stamped, and handed over our super-extra sealed letter to the counselor. I certainly forgot about the whole thing before we got back to our room.

A year later, I got mail. This was back when I was excited to get mail. It differed completely from today. Mail used to involve going outside. Today I hear the *ding* and the anxiety sets in while I imagine all sorts of bills that could be waiting for me. Although, it was kinda creepy to see a letter addressed to me in my handwriting. I eventually remembered what it was, but not what I had written.

Wasting no time, I ripped into the letter and was ready to hear my sage advice from my past self to my current self. I barely remembered most of the things I was concerned with in the letter. Some felt so insignificant. I was shocked I took the time to acknowledge them in a letter. With only the difference of time, so many of the big things had become forgotten things.

Joy is not a result of my situation, it is a frame of mind. It is the product of my attention. Whatever I focus on, becomes amplified, so I should focus carefully. Focus purposefully.

If I wrote the one-year-from-now Richard a note, would he even care about this thing? If not, do I need to invest any energy into it now? Can I remember that this too will pass?

Be curious, be kind, be whole, do good things.

Nine

Remote Start

"Instead of treating events as wins and losses, ask, *Did I learn something I can apply in the future?* If not, then you must treat it as a loss."

~ Naval Ravikant, Entrepreneur and Investor

Even at 1:00 a.m., Texas summer nights are hot, and the air is damp. We'd just left a club in the artsy music scene area of Dallas called Deep Ellum. Headed down Elm Street, I tossed my friend his car keys. After a bit of watching him fiddle with his remote, I felt a cocktail of anxiety, panic, and failure fill me.

He was in a band, and he rode to the club in their band van. I had driven down later in his car, which was a little Honda with a manual transmission. I followed the rule and safely parked, in first gear, just like I'd been taught. You are supposed to park a manual transmission in first gear—unless, of course, it has a remote start.

The club was warm, and outside wasn't refreshing. He wanted to start his car to get the AC cooling. As he fiddled with the remote, I was reminded of the remote start feature. By the time I found clarity, it was too late to stop him. I announced in a panic, "It's in gear!" as he pushed the button. My friend's eyes bloomed, and we took off jogging towards his car. An empty parking spot greeted us.

The Honda was nestled against the building across the alley. It had jumped over the parking stop, down the curb, across the alleyway, up another curb, and finally rested safely against the brick wall. I was very lucky that there was no damage to the car. We laughed the entire way home, imagining what the onlookers must have thought as they watched an empty car repeatedly lunging forward—this was way before autonomous, or self-driving, cars.

I tend to be afraid of making a mistake. Author Seth Godin has said we only need to avoid blunders, not mistakes.[14] Blunders are unrecoverable, mistakes are fixable. Mistakes are opportunities to learn and grow.

Can I stop being afraid of making an inevitable mistake? Do I learn from every event? Even the wins?

Be curious, be kind, be whole, do good things.

Ten

Socks

I am stubborn. It takes me a lot of work for me to form a habit, but when one locks in—it is very strong. My mom taught me to always turn my socks the "right way," so that we would leave the "outside" out. This approach lets the gross, dirty part that touched the ground have the most access to the soapy water. It was easiest to do this when I took the socks off to put them in the hamper. That way, after they were washed, the socks were all set to match and fold. It took strong, consistent parental coaching, and years of reminders from my mother and myself, but I mastered the method and built the habit. I found if I hooked my finger in the sock and slid, they stayed right side out.

After I was married, I noticed our washing machine would flip my socks inside out. It was the craziest thing. I was hypervigilant about taking my socks off right, but when I went to fold the socks, they were constantly inside out. Years went by of flipping these socks as I folded them. Late one night, we were watching TV and folding laundry. I asked my wife, "What's wrong with our washing machine? It turns socks inside out."

Surprise! It wasn't the machine. She was also raised to always flip socks the "right way," which meant inside out. This approach lets the gross, dirty part that touched the sweaty feet have the most access to the soapy water. She easily took her socks off like peeling a banana, preparing the sock to be washed "properly." She had been confused by my socks, never being ready to wash. For years, I was taking my socks off. Flipping them right side out. Robin was flipping them back inside out to wash. Then I would flip them the other way to fold. It was a slight inconvenience, but it was still a waste of time and energy.

Spending time to understand what happens before me and after me gives important context to what I do. I can try to create personal efficiencies, but they might disrupt the greater good.

Am I unintentionally complicating things that come after me? Can I curiously seek what is upstream and downstream from where I am? Will I continue to explore from there?

Be curious, be kind, be whole, do good things.

Eleven

Haunted

"Don't call people out. Call them in."

~ Loretta Ross, Civil Rights Activist

As a high school junior, I volunteered to work in a haunted house. My assignment was in the second to last scene. The last scene had no actors, so I was the last active scare. My job was to get the guests out towards the exit. When they came around the corner, I was their motivation to leave in the final two scenes. My tactic was to blend into the scenery, so they believed I was just a decorative creature. As they moved through the room, when it was too late to turn around, I announced my presence. Most often, I was greeted with crippling panic. As they froze, I'd sweep my arms from the side, encouraging them to move in the opposite direction.

Towards the end of another successful night, a young kid, maybe ten, came through alone. The stream of people kept me in a routine, and he fell right into my trap. I did what the Irish call *scared the bejesus out of him*. He was so panic-stricken that he sat down. He was done with this haunted house. Sobbing, not moving, he just sat. As his age sank in, I felt bad, and I wasn't sure what to do. I couldn't remove my makeup, so I took off my *monster* gloves and offered my *human* hand. He took it and stood up. I put my arm around his shoulder, and side-by-side we exited the rest of the way. He didn't realize how close to the end he was. But, even that close, he wouldn't have made it without an invitation.

When we find someone acting in a troublesome way, Loretta Ross suggests we invite them to grow instead of *calling them out*. Calling someone out assumes they know something they may not. This expectation is unfair and unhelpful. Instead, we should forgive them for the ignorance and encourage their growth.[15]

Sometimes I am the crying kid, stuck. Sometimes I am the helping hand. Always, I need to extend or accept a hand. Shoulder to shoulder is the most effective way to move forward together.

Am I offering you my hand? Am I accepting yours? Can I shine a light on a blind spot of my own or someone else?

Be curious, be kind, be whole, do good things.

Twelve

Shadows

"A stone cast a shadow across the ground. The shadow said: 'If it wasn't for this rock, I could get some sun.'"

~ James Richardson, *Vectors*

Throughout my life, I have been described as having an *old soul*. Perhaps it's my love of history, tracing the roots of things. It could also be because I am curmudgeonly. Often times, I can feel like an outsider because of my differences. As a response, sometimes I pretend to be something I think will blend in. When I try to be something I'm not, it feels weird. When I feel weird, I further distance from *fitting in*.

Sometimes I am the shadow. I waste time trying to will a change outside of my control. Or, embarrassed, I try to wish away the very thing that makes me who I am. Shame is rarely productive. Focusing on things outside of my control is an unwise investment of attention. Fitting in keeps me from standing out.

Am I trying to control things I can't control? Can I embrace what makes me who I am? If granted the wish, am I prepared to accept the new, rock-less version of myself?

Be curious, be kind, be whole, do good things.

Thirteen

Murder

I was an adult before I read anything by Agatha Christie. I am grateful I finally read her work, because her mysteries and feisty writing are fantastic. When I read *A Murder is Announced,* I saw a typo. In chapter 5, she called a primary character by the wrong name. Mrs. Blaylock was spelled Mrs. Blacklock. It was a harsh-looking, unfamiliar name, and I laughed out loud. Not as in lol, but an actual *out-loud* response. I felt some pride in finding this error. My edition is not an early printing, so it has had plenty of opportunities to be fixed, and it wasn't, and I found it.

But that was not what happened at all. I flipped through the previous chapters. Mrs. Blacklock was spelled out in every single instance. Every. Single. One.

It was an excellent reminder that I can know something, with absolute certainty, with *letter-to-the-editor* surety, and still be wrong.

Have I double-checked my understanding? Where can I be more curious? Am I listening to new information, learning, and revising my point of view?

Be curious, be kind, be whole, do good things.

Fourteen

Grand Theft Auto

As a teenager, I had recently earned my driver's license. I was in the phase where I would take every opportunity to go driving. One day, my mom sent me to the drugstore. As I came out of the store, I unlocked the door with my remote and settled into the car. I tried to start the engine, but the key wouldn't turn all the way. The key rotated one position. The car wouldn't start, but it rotated enough to power the radio. Unfamiliar music played. My first thought was a dead battery, but then I remembered the music playing.

My brain did that weird catch-up thing. Like on a Zoom call, when someone's video freezes for a few seconds. Then their audio and video rapidly speed through what they'd been saying in the interim. My brain unfroze, and I processed all the things I'd simultaneously experienced and missed. I had seen quite a few things but didn't let them register before dismissing them.

The car was parked crooked, the side mirrors and dashboard were the wrong color, and the driver's seat was too far forward. Oh crap! This was not my car. It looked a whole lot like my car, but it was not my car. My keyless remote unlocked the car, but it was not my car. My key slid into the ignition and turned, but this was NOT MY CAR!

I'm confident that if that car had started, I would have stolen a car that day.

The machine upstairs is always running. Sometimes I have to take a moment to make sure I am processing what's going on. I make mistakes without even noticing. Taking things as they are, without question, can overlook opportunities to improve. This attentiveness also allows me to fully experience and appreciate the moments happening now.

Can I tell when I am on autopilot? Am I experiencing life or just moving through? Can I be more alert? More intentional with my attention?

Be curious, be kind, be whole, do good things.

Fifteen

Stairs

"Do you have a head injury?" Yeah, probably.

Perhaps due to my odd sense of humor, but I have been asked this question an alarming number of times. Perhaps it should come as no surprise that I've knocked my noggin many times throughout my life, even as an adult.

The house where I spent most of my youth was a two-story house with a steep set of stairs. There was a landing and then the last step off to the side. At two or three years old, I had a toy horse with wheels. *Bucky* was a good horse. For twenty-ish years, I was told a story that I rode Bucky down the stairs. It was a fairly smooth ride until I put a head-shaped hole in the drywall at the landing. As an adult, it was revealed that my older sister was standing at the top of the stairs. She exclaimed, "I didn't do it!" I'm not sure the statute of limitations on attempted fratricide, but I'd appreciate a thorough investigation.

Unlike my rapid descent, I often think of approaching my work as a set of stairs. Too slow, too many distractions, and I'll never make it to the goal. Too fast, too busy, and I get exhausted and ineffective. Instead, there is a pace that seems to be ideal, to keep forward motion, but it is still one step at a time. At this pace, each step may not actually be easier than the last, but they each bring me closer to the goal.

Will I maintain momentum and just take the next step? Can I stop procrastinating and clear my distractions? I know what is next. Am I stepping up the stairs or staring up the steps?

Be curious, be kind, be whole, do good things.

Sixteen

Jokes

Standing at the front of a hotel banquet room, I had 100+ faces looking back at me. I was hosting a training session when we hit an unexpected gap in the agenda. With that many people in the room, it was very difficult to regain attention. We were trying to keep everything interesting and on a tight schedule.

The gap gave me some time to kill. Even just a few seconds can feel like an eternity, but luck was on my side. I remembered a joke and wedged it into a faux announcement. Deep breath.

"Oh, hey… just a reminder that Mother's Day is this coming Sunday. It is a great opportunity for you to recognize all the special women in your life. Please don't forget to share a token of appreciation. I remember my wife complained once when I didn't buy her flowers... but in my defense, I didn't know she sold flowers."

It is a slow roll across the room, but pretty quickly got a solid laugh from the room. Fast forward a month. A very smart, very capable co-worker approached me about that joke. She confided it made her feel really stupid.

She said, "I laughed when you told it, but I wasn't sure why. When everyone around me laughed, I was embarrassed that I didn't get it, so I went home and told it to a friend. They laughed. I told it to a parent at my kid's school. They laughed. I told it to my husband, and he laughed. Obviously, it was funny, but I did not get it."

She ultimately said that, once she broke it down, she saw the humor. I loved her courage in sharing this embarrassing moment. It also taught me or reminded me of at least two things:

- First, *Communication is hard.* Sometimes we hear what was said and react. We can repeat what was said and get a reaction, yet still not understand what it is we were hearing. This can lead to copying others, but not understanding why.

- Second, *Moving along with the group is easy.* Sometimes we react in a certain way because everyone else does. Without even thinking for ourselves, we react/respond in the way we see around us. This is dangerous, because people see a group and assume they are right. They assume the group knows what they are doing, but some groups are just moving as a herd.

Can I explore and turn an idea around to see how to fully understand it? How can I make sure I am heard and understood? How can I ensure I understand you? Are these my real thoughts and feelings or just how I *think* I am *supposed* to respond? Am I willing to share my mistakes so others can learn and grow?

Be curious, be kind, be whole, do good things.

Seventeen

Crossroads

Led Zeppelin, the Rolling Stones, the Beatles, and many others have played Robert Johnson's songs and list him as a key influence. Johnson lived a big, but short life. He hailed from Mississippi and died at the age of twenty seven after drinking poison in a bottle of whiskey in 1938.

Biographers described early Johnson as charismatic, but "embarrassingly bad" at the guitar. He disappeared for about six months and came back as a powerhouse and highly influential musician. He was such a force that a legend began during his life that persists today. The legend says that Johnson, a rejected musician, stood at the crossroads on the way out of town and cried out for help. His desire to be successful conjured the devil, and he sold his soul at the crossroads for the talent he returned with.

Researchers learned that during the six-month hiatus from public view, Johnson was relentlessly practicing. He played along to records and studied. His teacher wasn't allowed to play guitar at home, so they practiced in the local graveyard, which probably gave rise to the myth. Johnson fully embraced the story with his song "Cross Road Blues."

Setting aside the supernatural aspects, we often find ourselves at crossroads. The fork in the road is scary when we are staring down a big decision. I sometimes delay, perhaps because I don't want to face the risk of failing. I must remember that not making a decision is a decision. The best things in life take work. When I'm given the opportunity between two things, I should probably take the more challenging one.

Am I willing to put in the work? Can I delay less and jump in faster? Will I commit to my passion so fully that it seems supernatural?

Be curious, be kind, be whole, do good things.

Eighteen

Walking

"I had the *right* to remain silent, but I did not have the *ability*."

~ Ron White, Comedian

When I was a child, I was difficult to parent. As you hear that, I suspect very little middle ground. Either you thought, "What?!? That's crazy," or, "Yeah, duh." Either way, I made it to adulthood and still work hard to control my verbal and facial responses.

In this situation, I was old enough to drive, but not mature enough to bite my tongue. My parents grounded me from driving. I don't recall what I did, but, as always, I looked for loopholes. This grounding only involved the car; I was allowed to leave. So, I walked to see my girlfriend. She lived fifteen miles away, twenty minutes by car–several hours on foot. I set out in sandals with a half-bottle of water and the fiery persistence of an ornery teenager.

As the determination wore off, the walk became increasingly difficult. Several times I tried to find an alternative, but I was already past the halfway point, so turning around was not smart. The woods between our houses didn't have any cars to flag down. I was exhausted and dehydrated. It was getting dark, and I'd been chewed up by the bugs that haunt Texas summers. By the time I got there, I could barely walk.

The most challenging part of the walk was the voice in my head telling me I could not finish. About two-thirds through, I slowed down and scolded myself. But distracting myself with the discomforts and complaints was not helping me accomplish what I had committed to do. Self-sabotage is often my number one enemy. Sometimes it is enough to just tell yourself that you can. If you can get at least halfway, then finishing is easier than turning back.

How often is my inner critic the biggest, or only, obstacle to accomplishing something? If I am here and committed, why not finish what I've started? Is the struggle capability or willingness? Can my inner critic become my inner advocate?

Be curious, be kind, be whole, do good things.

Nineteen

Chewie

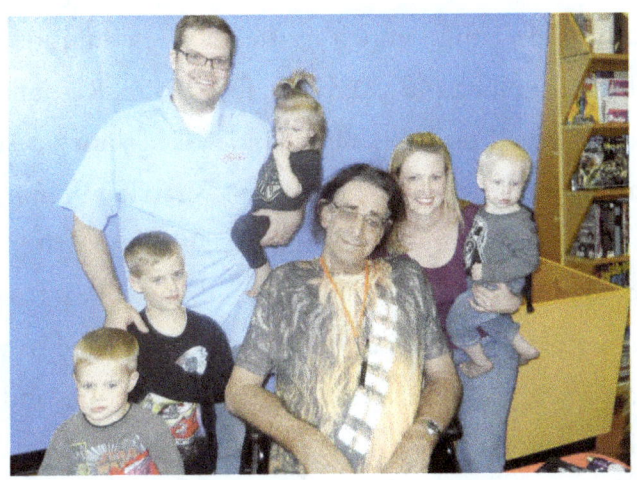

We have four kids and they were all under six years old. Our favorite comic book store is Zeus Comics, and they were hosting Free Comic Book Day, an annual event where they host comic book artists, writers, and other celebrities (mark your calendar on the first Saturday in May). We had been many times before, but the attendance was exceptionally high that year due to all of the interesting people Zeus comics had at the store.

Our reason for being there was Peter Mayhew. Peter played Chewbacca in Star Wars and our entire family are big fans. Unfortunately, it was extra hot and the line of people snaked the entire shopping center. Once we got through the door, another line was wrapping around the store, waiting for us. We had waited in line to get into the store, so we could then... wait in line. The older boys were confused because they typically got to browse at Zeus, but we were just standing there this time. At least we had made it inside and were finally enjoying the air conditioning.

Once we were about 25 percent through this second line, someone came to us and asked who we were there to see. We shared our love for Star Wars and that we were there to meet "Mr. Mayhew." The guy simply said, "Cool," and took off. I didn't think much of it until a few minutes later when someone else approached and asked us to follow him. Responsible for the safety of my platoon, I probably should have asked some questions, but I didn't because I was just glad to be moving. We followed him all the way through the store to the very front of the line. When we arrived, Peter said, "You sure have your hands full!" This is something we hear frequently. He continued, "I am grateful you came, but you don't need to wait in this line." He took pictures with us and signed promo pictures and books. We made small talk, but mostly he made our day.

Our children were excited by the store and people in costume. They were a little too young to know why we were patiently waiting in line. Chewbacca has always been one of our Star Wars favorites. His whole life is in service to those around him. The character was clearly rooted in Peter's approach to life. He didn't have to break the rules and let us skip. However, it made a lasting impression. This small act of kindness on his part improved our day, it gave us a story to tell, and it forever changed how I look at *rules*.

Process and procedure are important. However, sometimes it is more important to understand the specific situation and circumstances. If we deeply understand the rules and their intention, we can cautiously step around them when necessary and still fulfill that intent.

Where do I let formality get in the way of being helpful? Where can I offer generosity and kindness to move everything and everyone forward? Can I simplify and still accomplish the task? Who needs my kindness and attention right now?

Be curious, be kind, be whole, do good things.

Twenty

Corners

A father was outside working when he realized he couldn't see his young son. Panic hit as each place he checked turned up empty. Time slowed and fear increased with every passing minute. His heart raced as he ran out of places to check. He went down the street; his son was nowhere to be found.

Finally, he rounded the corner to find his son playing with his toy truck. The dad's adrenaline turned the fear into anger. He grabbed his son's arm and loudly said, "How many times do I have to tell you, don't go past the corner?!?"

The boy nervously asked, "Daddy, what's a corner?"[16]

Anger is most often rooted in fear. Fear is an anticipation of something that may or may not happen. This fear takes many forms, such as fear of missing out, failure, or rejection. I have lived no one's life but my own. I shouldn't assume others know what I know. Being present and clear communication can reduce the feeling of fear. Fear, like hope, can only exist in the future. Being mindful of my current situation, I can more often choose hope over fear.

Can I remember I am likely not mad, but just scared? Will my first goal be to understand and then to be understood? Can I communicate better? Will I choose hope over fear as I seek to be in this moment?

Be curious, be kind, be whole, do good things.

Twenty-One

Farmers

Do the clocks *fall forward* or *fall back*? Either way, when the clocks shift by an hour, maybe we should just pick our favorite direction.

Like many, I find the time change to be a painful semiannual annoyance. It was especially obnoxious when our children were younger and we had to manage their naps and bedtimes. Not sure why I care, but it is Daylight Saving Time and *not* Daylight Saving*s* Time (DST). Either way, I had always heard that it was instituted to support the farmers. The shifting of hours gave them more daylight. Based on a non-scientific, tiny sampling, this belief had a 100 percent hit rate on everyone I polled. It's also completely inaccurate.

Farmers are not responsible for DST. They actually lobbied against the legislature. The change in time is excruciating for them. It causes disruption in the morning to get crops to market, and as difficult as it is to shift your schedule, imagine trying to retrain the livestock. DST has been polarizing since its inception but originated to conserve energy during World War I. The U.S. did not consistently adopt it until LBJ (mostly) standardized it in 1966. Even today, some places opt out of the headache.

As far as I can recall, I have always blamed the farmers, and I am not alone. Yet neither the length of time I have believed it nor the number of people who also believe it makes it true. Learning this reminds me I have biases I don't even realize. My deeply held beliefs, formed through System 1 thinking, things people I trusted taught me, and *facts* that seem to be generally accepted may not actually be true. Curiosity helps me challenge what I think might be the truth. Being open to change, to growing, to learning new things should be my default. Changing my mind, especially when getting further information, is a good thing.

It is more likely that I need to confirm something that I am most confident in *knowing*. Where else might I sincerely feel I am right, but may not be? Do I have an open mind? Will I change my mind?

Be curious, be kind, be whole, do good things.

P.S. I still don't like DST, but I publicly apologize to all farmers I've disparaged over the years.

Twenty-Two

M&Ms

I was camping with my two older sons. They were very young. Chase is about three years older than Ryan. Chase shared that snacks were his favorite part of camping. Ryan replied that he loved trail mix because it has "Nimanims."

Chase kindly corrected Ryan, saying, "They are called M *and* Ns." Not to miss a laugh, I told them I picked out all the Ns. So, if they look carefully, our mix only had Ms, and some misprinted Ws.

Their conversation was loving, but they approached it as right and wrong, even at a very young age. And, by that standard, they were both wrong. When I think about how we argue or debate, we describe an argument as war. Debates have winners and losers. We "attack their position," "cover our bases," and "defend our own." We "shoot down arguments." If we "fall behind" in the debate, we are "losing ground." Conversations shouldn't be battlefields. We aren't at war. We are just sharing our understanding.

In *Greenlights*, Matthew McConaughey recounts a heated discussion between two locals at a bar in Africa. After listening for a moment, Matthew sided with one man, referring to him as "right." The person he supported chastised him, who exclaimed, "It's not about right or wrong, it's about 'Do you understand?'"

Matthew apologized, and the person he'd sided against sternly said, "You'd better be different, not sorry."

When I am in a discussion, I naturally consider myself right and the other person wrong. I sometimes feel like I need to *win*. Instead, I should approach it as a conversation. I am working to understand them and then help them understand me. Right and wrong rarely allow us to be better. Besides, we might both be wrong. Or better, we might both be right, just in different ways.

Am I generously listening? Can I seek deep understanding? How can I find common ground?

Be curious, be kind, be whole, do good things.

Twenty-Three

Change

A child complained to his mother about the hardships and struggles in his life. He felt that just as he resolved one, another would pop up in its place. The mother put three pots of water on the stove. She placed potatoes, eggs, and coffee beans separately in each pot.

After the water boiled, the mother peeled the eggs and placed them on a plate with the potatoes. Then she poured coffee into a mug. Finally, she told her son, "You can be the potato, the egg, or the coffee bean." The boy was confused and asked for clarification. "All three faced the same challenging pot of hot water—the potato was firm and became soft, the egg was a thin hard shell with a liquid interior that became hard, but the coffee beans changed the water itself and became something new."[17]

Challenges, difficulties, and adversity are a part of life. I cannot avoid them, but I can decide if I want to be a potato, an egg, or the coffee.

Are you faced with challenges? Can you create something new with yourself and your surroundings? If not you, who? If not now, when?

Be curious, be kind, be whole, do good things.

Twenty-Four

Oatmeal

The Quaker Oats Company advertises a "heart healthy" instant oatmeal, but focus groups showed that Quaker was missing out on a segment of customers because of the high sugar content. They set their food scientists on the mission of reducing the amount of sugar per packet of oatmeal. The obvious answer would be artificial sweeteners, but taste panels rejected the flavor. The scientists were stuck. Eventually, they found a solution that would maintain flavor and reduce sugar content by 35 percent.[18]

Their solution was to replace a small amount of real sugar with an artificial sweetener while keeping the taste profile. Then they reduced the overall serving size by 27 percent. So now, for the same price, you can get reduced sugar oatmeal primarily due to portion control. Want the same great taste with less sugar? Eat less.

As a side note, I learned the "strawberries" and "peaches" are actually dehydrated apples, and the "blueberries" are dehydrated figs.

Sometimes the best way to solve a problem is to change course altogether. When we look at things from different angles and hear multiple points of view, we can increase our creativity in tackling the challenges we face.

When I face a challenge: Do I need to zoom out? Zoom in? Turn it over? Can I ask an expert? A fresh perspective from a beginner? Do I even need a solution or just a change in my approach?

Be curious, be kind, be whole, do good things.

Twenty-Five

Sewing

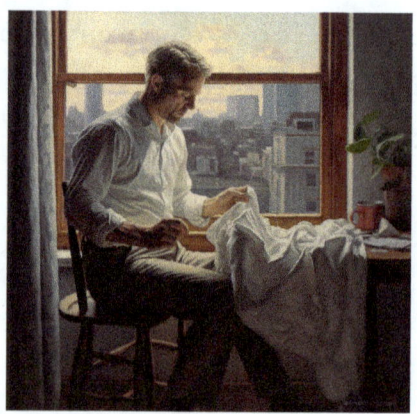

I purchased several new dress shirts to wear to the office. After I removed the thirty-seven clips, tags, stickers, collar stays, and other paraphernalia, I noticed a button was loose. My mom taught me how to sew as a child. With a few quick loops and a triple knot, all was well.

Carefully avoiding a needle-based injury, I found myself grateful for my mom and for the sewing kit. Without the training and the supplies, I wouldn't have been able to fix my issue quickly. I am especially glad that I did not have to forge a needle, nor did I have to grow cotton and then spin it into thread.

I very much enjoy the sense of being self-sufficient, but even in those moments, I highly depend on my community. We need our neighbors where we live and where we work. We need to contribute our strengths, talents, and capabilities. When my needs are met, I should then tend to my neighbors.

Am I appreciating my community? How badly would I struggle if I were truly on my own? Can I be depended on? Will I ask for help when I need it? Am I serving my community?

Be curious, be kind, be whole, do good things.

Twenty-Six

Ghost Stories

My family spent the weekend in San Antonio for my oldest child's high school marching band competition. We stayed at the *haunted* Menger Hotel, a 150-year-old establishment that is proud of its many famous visitors, including President Teddy Roosevelt's recruitment of Rough Riders at the hotel bar.

Like some older buildings, the hotel has accumulated stories of the ghosts of previous guests. The side door of the hotel directly faces the Alamo, adding to those stories. We stayed one floor below the *most haunted* floor. The owners have added many additions to the hotel throughout its history, so it has various styles. You can get lost in the winding corridors. At one point, while wrapping around the fifth floor, you are suddenly on the third floor.

We stayed up late one night to walk through the haunted floor. While collecting everyone in the lobby, I noticed our youngest son wrestling with something. We sat quietly for a minute, then I asked him how he was feeling. He told me he doesn't "necessarily believe in ghosts." However, he *was* concerned that he might still get scared, which would likely lead to bad dreams.

After another minute, he shared what was really bothering him, "I am afraid that I will get made fun of for saying I don't want to go."

That struck me hard. This clearly took him a lot of courage. It was also a simple thing for me to resolve. I told everyone else, "We are tired and are gonna head to bed. Y'all have fun."

A couple of hours later, the rest of the crew came back to the room, and we all settled in for the night. At 2:00 a.m. our middle son sat up, loudly talking in his sleep. I went to quiet him, and he DOVE on his brother. I was afraid that one of them was hurt.

I checked on them, and I encouraged him to lie back down. "You are talking in your sleep. Get back to your side of the bed."

His eyes popped open. Terror suddenly filled them, and he screamed, "AHHH! It's the ghost!!!"

I realized one child was worried about speaking up but found his voice. He slept like a champ. The other had a terrible night's rest. Sometimes we do things we don't want to, just because we fear judgment from speaking up.

We might even put ourselves through misery to avoid the discomfort of speaking up.

Am I advocating for myself? Do I create an environment where others feel comfortable sharing their discomfort? Can I do the big thing for someone else that is small for me?

Be curious, be kind, be whole, do good things.

Twenty-Seven

Inviting

I spent ten years on an advisory committee for a charitable organization that helped feed, clothe, and financially stabilize those in need. This was a life-changing opportunity. It forced me to learn how to influence through inviting and enticing. I witnessed people experiencing significant challenges while I went through my own series of trials. These experiences led to significant moments of personal growth. In the work, our challenge was to meet people's basic needs and give them a foundation to ultimately support themselves.

Nearly everyone I worked with had volunteered for a long time. Like many things we do for a while, the autopilot sets in, and it can become easy to lose focus on our mission. One night, my fellow volunteers were discussing our frustration with those being served because they weren't following through on their commitments. The discussion turned harsh about those we were there to help. Chris, a long-time volunteer, said: "Let's not forget that door is the heaviest door in the world."

He meant the door that those needing help had to enter. I knew firsthand how heavy those doors were. I struggled to open similar doors. Asking for help can be incredibly difficult.

Will I remember my struggles? Do I know where the heavy doors are? Am I willing to pass through? Will I hold them open for someone else?

Be curious, be kind, be whole, do good things.

Twenty-Eight

Different

Apple made commotion in marketing with their slogan *Think Different*. Their intention was to encourage us to go about our lives differently than before, but I also feel an implied "embrace that we think differently from each other." In a conversation with a friend, it startled me to learn that I think differently. My thinking method, as in the literal way I experience thoughts in my head, differs from how other people think.

Most of the time, my brain processes thoughts like an old radio show—characters, sound effects, and poorly defined plots. It is rare that I visualize my thoughts, but the audio content is rich. Unlike an old radio, I can rewind and fast forward. I can replay things over and over, the same or with slight changes. I can predict what's next by replaying the prediction with different outcomes. Little vignettes. Nearly constantly. The vivid nature of my made-up thoughts creates genuine emotions about people and scenarios that never played out.

This manufactured ill will has been a stumbling block throughout my life. Most often, it involves getting angry with someone based on a conversation in my head that did not really take place. I get frustrated before we ever start our interaction in life. I come with the hostility from my make-believe fight. Which, by the way, I won… most of the time.

Will that change for me? Probably not much. Instead, I try to use those natural tendencies to improve my life and the experience of those around me. Scenario planning helps me maintain balance. It fuels my sense of humor and helps me process emotion before I experience it. It allows me to appreciate being in the moment. Being present.

Humans often desire to change. I used to think I needed to erase my shortcomings. I would have to shed any attributes that got in my way. Completely abandon the things I trip on. I'm learning, albeit slowly, that the change needed is to use our traits, our entire selves, for the betterment of our life and the lives of those around us. I can embrace my quirks in unique, yet productive ways. This has given new meaning to the generic platitude, "Turn your weakness into strengths." This bar is attainable. It isn't easy, but it is possible.

Can I be patient with myself when I try to change something I've had my whole life? Will I have a realistic plan and forgive myself along the way? Can I think differently?

Be curious, be kind, be whole, do good things.

Twenty-Nine

Pistol Shrimp

I recently learned about the Pistol Shrimp. It is shaped similar to a crawfish or a three-inch lobster–except one claw is huge. The big claw is over an inch long, about half its body length. If they lose their big claw, it severs a nerve that triggers growth hormones and the small claw grows to become the big claw. Then they regrow a new small claw where the big one was.

When a pistol shrimp detects prey, the big claw opens and a chamber in the claw fills up with water. It snaps the claw shut and shoots a water bubble out at sixty miles per hour! The snapping of the claw is louder than a shotgun (210 decibels), and it occasionally produces light from the snap. The light from the collapsing bubble is hotter than the sun's surface (7,700* versus the sun at 5,500*).

Every time I share the pistol shrimp discovery with someone, they exhibit disbelief until they look it up for themselves. When we learn something new, it really is a discovery, sometimes equipped with the satisfying ah-ha feeling. There are so many fascinating things in the universe–some of them are less *discovered* than the rest. Skepticism of new things can be warranted, but too much can impede exploration, learning, and trying new things.

How can I keep an open mind? Can I try something new or retry something I've left behind? How can I learn and apply this to enrich my own life and pursuits?

Be curious, be kind, be whole, do good things.

Thirty

Ping

Ping, ping, ping.

My oldest son lost his AirPod again. AirPod, singular, because a dog had already chewed its mate. Wireless earbuds are convenient, but corded headphones seem harder to lose. Maybe we should put a string on the wireless earbuds.

If you misplace them, the iPhone lets you send an audible *ping* to previously connected AirPods. "Ping, ping, ping." In his search, he moved throughout the house, trying to quiet everyone and everything. The faintness of sound made it hard to pinpoint, but he knew it was nearby. He headed to various rooms, then upstairs. After about ten minutes, I noticed the sound was nearly impossible to hear from where I was.

I found him rifling through his room, and it was louder again. "Chase, I can only hear it near you. Check your pockets." He had already checked there but, after searching him again, we found it in the hood of his hoodie. He kept hearing the faint ping, but it never got louder, so he assumed it was further away.

I can laugh, but out of empathy as I've been in similar situations more times than I can count. Often, when I'm in pursuit of something, I get so caught up in seeking that I fail to pause along the way. It is common to find what I am looking for right under my nose. Frequently, my spouse finds the missing item in the junk drawer after I've gone through it ten times. Sitting right on top, somehow disappearing into the noise of the drawer or even the hunt itself.

The solution might be attentiveness. Sometimes I check items off my list too quickly. I get pulled by the pursuit of *finishing*. I walk through the plan instead of accomplishing the mission.

Am I paying attention and adjusting along the way? Am I being mindful of my surroundings? What am I seeking that is right there? What am I missing that may already be under my nose or in my hoodie?

Be curious, be kind, be whole, do good things.

Thirty-One

Learning

I love to read. Unless I am supposed to. Recommend a book and I get to read it when I want to? No problem. Tell me I have to read a book as an assignment? I will spend hours rereading the same paragraph, then suddenly realize I need to dust. Or organize my sock drawer.

During the pandemic, like most American families, my children shifted to *distance learning*. It was abrupt, so they checked the essential regulatory boxes to qualify as learned. Watching them helped me remember how difficult it is to be forced to learn. We were lucky to have outstanding teachers who worked extremely hard to help our children learn. Most importantly, to help our children *want* to learn.

This resistance is so common that we reflect it in how we talk about learning. We *take a course* or *take lessons*, much like we *take medicine*, or my grandparents would say, "Take our lumps." This isn't how we should describe learning. Learning is a process we get to experience, something we get to be a part of. It is a unique and novel experience that can break the monotony of routine. We can discover efficiency. We can develop new talents or skills. Learning opens doors and creates an appreciation for things we don't understand. Learning sheds light on more opportunities to learn.

Do I choose to learn? Am I open to conversation? Will I test things? Can I accept that I only fail if I don't learn?

Be curious, be kind, be whole, do good things.

Thirty-Two

Mood

Max with his mom and sister and his new car.

October reminds me of my grandparents. My parents' magic and costume store was the busiest during October, so my sisters and I became transients. We'd either sleep at the store or move between our grandparents' houses.

My mom's dad, Max, was one of the most interesting people I have ever known. Max's father (also Max) was 73 when my grandfather was born and died four years later. My grandpa had various jobs growing up. He was an "office boy" for Butler Brothers when one of his bosses handcuffed a suitcase to his wrist and gave him an address. When he got there he found it was full of cash, which they hid underground just days before the start of the Great Depression. He also delivered bread for Manor Bakers. One of his stops was the Parker's house (Bonnie Parker's mom, of Bonnie and Clyde).

At fourteen, he'd saved up enough money to buy a car, but the dealership wouldn't sell it to him because he was too young. So, he went to the Red-Light district and hired a prostitute to buy the car on his behalf. So, it was just Max with his mom and sister and his new car. Max was always the happiest person in any room. He was frugal, but generous. He loved to give things away–from candy to cash.

Max owned a lot of residential real estate and tended to all the properties. One day, in his red truck (not the car the prostitute bought for him), we headed to a property in Corsicana, Texas. Since we'd be on the road for a while, he brought lunch. We each had a bottle of Dr. Pepper, his with a bag of peanuts dropped in. I ate a pack of those orange peanut butter crackers, the kind where the cracker is DayGlo orange.

We went into one apartment, and he put me in front of the TV with a kid I'd never met and don't recall ever seeing again. After about an hour, we were back on the road. It was an unexpectedly brief trip, and there wasn't any of the typical manual labor involved. I was curious why we even went. He said that this tenant was struggling to pay rent, and she'd called asking for help. They went through her financials together, made a plan, and he adjusted her rent so she could get her life back on track. I often think of this and his countless kind gestures.

He grew up during the Great Depression with a single (twice-widowed) mom and seven siblings. He experienced two world wars, lost a child at birth, then a few years later lost his wife and another child at birth. His life was filled with physical, emotional, and financial crises. Yet, he was always kind, generous, and happy.

Grandpa showed me we can't always choose our circumstances, but we can choose our disposition. He chose kindness, and it was infectious. I occasionally run into people who knew him. They often tell me they "loved the Candy Man." Many of us look for opportunities to help other people. When we have the ability to help, we should. On the flip side, people want to help. When I need help, it is okay to ask. When offered, I should accept it.

My circumstances don't have to affect my mood. Can I choose a kinder, or happier, disposition? Am I asking for help when I need it and accepting others' offers to assist? Will I seek opportunities to support those around me?

Be curious, be kind, be whole, do good things.

Thirty-Three

Wrecked

I was in the left turn lane at a red light. It was a busy intersection, and we'd been at the stoplight for a couple of minutes. My mind was wandering while waiting for the green light. WHAM!

If you've ever been rear-ended, you know the pattern. I heard it before realizing I'd also felt it. Confusion followed by a rush of adrenaline. The adrenaline made me shake. Then, finally, I started assessing the situation, the damage, and deciding what to do next. It wasn't safe to stay where we were, so we completed the turn and found a parking lot.

The other driver had just moved to this area from across the Dallas metroplex. He was headed to his first day of work and was very nervous about the new job. There was more traffic than he expected, and he was running a little late. He'd checked his navigation on his phone and hit the brakes too late. After checking on each other's well-being, we swapped insurance and contact info.

I'd been in three accidents in ten years. All three times, I was rear-ended while sitting completely stopped. Every time, I had been still long enough that getting hit was a complete surprise. Terrible, week-altering surprises. Pardon my language, but I'm getting sick of it, I tell you, pretty darn sick of it.

This time I felt sorry for the other driver and immediately chose to be as kind as possible. Many times, I have nearly been the other driver that hit someone. I was lucky in my misses. We weren't as lucky that night. But accidents happen. I controlled what I could control. Every person around us had their own story for that day. They were headed to a new job in the office, meeting a friend for dinner, or any number of other places coming from or going to. We are not stuck in traffic. We are traffic.

When can I choose kindness despite inconvenience? Where should I pay better attention? Can I embrace whatever happens as an opportunity to grow?

Be curious, be kind, be whole, do good things.

Thirty-Four

Oh Well

Driving to work, it played again. The song was amazing, but I wasn't sure what it was. I'd heard it on the radio five or six times over the last decade, but I had never been able to identify the song. At the office, I complained to a friend of mine. He's a musician and tried to help me but didn't recognize it from the minor parts I remembered. He suggested I check the radio station's website because they post all the songs they have played within the last twenty-four hours. I saved a copy of the webpage and that night I headed to YouTube.

I went through the list. Since I grew up listening to this genre I knew most of the bands on the list, I was able to cut out a lot of the titles and go straight to playing all the songs from bands that I didn't recognize. After several hours of picking through the songs and coming up dry, I got very frustrated and considered crazy thoughts like *maybe they forgot to list this one*. Or *maybe I didn't actually hear it*. Or perhaps it was a memory from the day before and I had missed the twenty-four-hour window.

I was annoyed, but I'd invested too much time to give up. I called on my tenacity and restarted my search, going song by song, even listening to the songs from bands I knew. Previously, I had skipped songs and artists I was very familiar with. For instance, Stevie Nicks' voice was so recognizable that I knew it wasn't Fleetwood Mac and didn't need to listen to their songs.

However, what I didn't know was that the first version of the Fleetwood Mac band had a very different sound and didn't include Stevie Nicks. I was unaware of this fact and made judgments based on assumptions I had made from my limited understanding (bias). It turns out that the song I was looking for was on radio station's list after all. It was "Oh Well (Pt.1)" from the original Fleetwood Mac band, and now I put it on nearly every playlist I create.

I had wrongly held assumptions. I used that to make decisions on what to listen to and what to skip. I tried to take a shortcut and ended up spending even more time than just doing the work in the first place. Shortcuts only work if I know where I am going. Or if I am okay only going where the shortcut does.

What am I missing out on because I *know* something is *true*? Where am I being biased/ignorant? Can I be more curious to learn and understand?

Be curious, be kind, be whole, do good things.

Thirty-Five

Hood

My lane of traffic was crawling and the lanes next to me were moving too fast for me to safely get out of the slow lane. As I approached the slow-moving obstruction, I saw that there was an accident and a brand-new Bronco with a wrecked front end was causing the slow-down. The wreck had obviously occurred recently, because the driver was still visibly rattled. They were driving very slowly in the left lane, but not pulling over. I am guessing they had been driving for a while, because the vehicle they hit was nowhere to be seen.

The accident had disabled the hood's latch, causing it to cover the windshield. The anxious driver was using the narrow gap between the bottom of the hood and the dashboard to navigate. They were unable to see well, driving a heavily damaged vehicle, at an unsafe speed. They probably should have pulled over to the shoulder and called for help. Adrenaline was probably still pumping from the accident, and the limited visibility made their situation worse.

A high-emotion environment will invoke our fight-or-flight response. As a result, we often make choices that we probably wouldn't make with a clear head. In those situations, I am best served by taking a pause. It may seem like my options are limited to those presented during my initial panic, but often there are more paths available.

Have I taken time to see clearly and weigh my options? Am I acknowledging that I am not stuck in traffic, I am traffic? Am I breathing?

Be curious, be kind, be whole, do good things.

Thirty-Six

Falling

I was running a little late to a meeting and, while torturing myself for not being on time, I took the stairs. As I rounded the landing between floors, I found a crew with two full loads of metal pipes on carts like the ones you use at Home Depot to haul plywood. One of the workers stumble-stepped backward, bumping into one of the carts. This shifted the load, and the cart rolled toward the stairs. Unfortunately, he grabbed the cart too late, and it rolled onto the stairs, tipping its load and pulling him with it, right in my direction.

I don't remember thinking anything, but I sprinted up the steps to stop him and the cart from running me over. A couple of pipes fell, but we averted any serious disaster.

The cart rolling toward the stairs suggested the brake wasn't engaged. Sometimes, to save a few seconds, we can end up costing ourselves much more than time. Some corners are not worth cutting. After avoiding disaster, I felt silly about being stressed out about being a few minutes late to a meeting. Life has a way of re-prioritizing our focus. While I want to do a good job, I need to invest my emotions wisely.

What should I remember is just *small stuff*? What corners should I avoid cutting? Which corners need to be trimmed?

Be curious, be kind, be whole, do good things.

Thirty-Seven

Rose

"We don't have problems. We have *opportunities*." I have heard this saying so many times it isn't just stale; it has lost its soul. Is the advice to rename my weaknesses strengths? Simply changing the name of something doesn't change what it is. In Shakespeare's play, Juliet shares a similar sentiment.

> "What's in a name? That which we call a rose
> By any other name would smell as sweet;
> So Romeo would, were he not Romeo call'd"

~ *Romeo and Juliet* (Act 2, Scene 2)

I love to read, but I struggle with it. Sometimes I lack focus or desire. Sometimes I want to read something different. Or I am too tired, too obligated, or too many things fighting against me. I convinced myself I wasn't suited to be a *reader*. It was too difficult for me. I didn't have time or just didn't feel like reading what was available. I realized I was only falling short of what I thought a *reader* was supposed to be. I decided to shed the old definition.

I gave myself permission to read as little as I wanted. I might read one paragraph, then stop. It was okay to start a book, decide it was not for me, and quit reading it—sometimes forever. I was allowed to start reading one book, then another, then another before finishing any of the books. It was okay to read fiction, non-fiction, self-help, etc. In fact, I've started reading stuff I know nothing about simply because of a recommendation by a friend.

I have reading piles near my go-to reading spots. Each book is in various states of being consumed. At times, I will sit and read an entire book. Other times, I'll just read a chapter or a paragraph. Some nights I read one sentence, realize I picked the wrong book for that night, and choose another or just go to bed. Once I cracked the code to reading in my unique way, I regained my love of reading. I now read and retain more. Then, of course, I had to learn how to take notes in my unique way.

Everything I read becomes a part of me. It gives me tools, skills, and methods for solving problems I haven't run into yet. It gives me potential connection points to relate to others in ways I'm not yet aware of. My *problems* of focus and discipline become genuine opportunities of breadth and variety. These skills feed my relentless curiosity. I did not resolve my difficulties with reading by calling my problem an opportunity. I resolved the issue by redefining what I want to accomplish and accommodating my particular way with a practical reframing of my approach. I read how I read, and I accept that.

When I am frustrated by *problems*, I try this pivot. Sometimes it is about redefining what I should be. I rarely need to become someone different. Rather, I need to leverage my unique skills to become more of myself.

Where else can I reframe or reuse my problems/shortcomings to be a real-world, hands-on opportunity? Where else do I have an unnecessary definition of what I *should* be? Can I accept that what I am is sufficient, then build from there? Is the problem me or the label I attached?

Be curious, be kind, be whole, do good things.

Thirty-Eight

Boom

Have you ever done anything stupid? Lol. I narrowly dodged an injury from an explosion. Growing up, television frequently warned us: "Kids, don't try this at home." I did not try it at home. I went to a friend's house.

Like many of my fellow scouts, I was obsessed with fire. We burnt things. I'd heard if a Black Cat firecracker was flat in your palm, it would sting but not do significant damage. However, if you closed your fist around the firecracker, you'd lose your fingers. I was unwilling to experiment with that directly; however, I had a better idea.

We found that match heads burned fast and created a lot of pressure. We clipped the heads off about 100 matches and crammed them into a Bubble

Tape container (similar to a can of Copenhagen). To ensure it held, we wrapped it in a lot of duct tape. For the fuse we daisy-chained a handful of fuses from a pack of Black Cats together. To ensure we maximized the pressure, we dug a foot-deep hole in his backyard. We lit the fuse and waited for what seemed like ten minutes... KA-BOOM!

We could feel the sound. Dirt clouded the air and peppered our faces. A wad of grass landed next to me. For the grand finale, two full panels of fence snapped off at the ground and fell into the alley with a thud.

Our experiment could have ended far worse, but it wasn't for nothing; we learned about safety, force, pressure, and fence repair. I suppose we were dancing a fine line between stupid and curious. Aside from these types of shenanigans, my curiosity has really served me well throughout my life.

Being curious has given me a small understanding of many topics. It is easier to find intersections with other people's interests, and my curiosity has created a toolkit of potential solutions for problems I've not yet encountered. Curious exploring has given me ample opportunities to learn how to make mistakes. And then learn from those mistakes. Curiosity feeds into creativity–the more tools/skills I have available, the less dependent I am on traditional approaches. I am certain we all have this innate curiosity and are mistakenly taught to stop asking questions and tamp it down.

Can I ask more *whys* and *hows*? Will I explore the unknown? Am I willing to play?

Be curious, be kind, be whole, do good things.

Thirty-Nine

Blocks

The initial version of each of these essays came into existence as a weekly correspondence. Each week they flowed relatively easily. I'd make notes and suggestions as I pondered an idea or ran into an issue. Luckily, the topics seemed to surface themselves. I superstitiously worried that I might hit writer's block; and then it struck.

The ideas came so easily that the first week something didn't immediately come to mind, I got in my head. I started working that I was done. I had written everything I knew and there was nothing left to give.

I looked at a blank page for several hours and finally resigned myself to bed, in hopes that something would strike the next morning. I put my laptop away and then thought about the advice many professional writers give: if you want to write, then write. If you don't start writing, you will get stuck in a continued loop of *not starting*. Writer's block can only occur when you are not writing, so write.

I sometimes find myself stuck in the writer's block of life. Staring at a blank screen. The solution is to just go. When we have a task list that is paralyzing us, the best thing to do is roll up our sleeves. Do the work. Start at number 1 and do it.

Where am I stuck, not starting? Do I know the first step? Will I take it? When in doubt, do.

Be curious, be kind, be whole, do good things.

Forty

Loss

A coworker, who was also a friend, who was my age, with children my kids' ages, unexpectedly passed away on a work trip. It was a raw, but pure attempt to share my heart as best as I could at the time.

Crushing. Tragic. Devastating.

These weak words. They may be the strongest I have at the moment. They fall so short.

"We lost someone." He isn't lost. We know where he is. Or was.

He may not be lost, but he is gone. Certainly, he won't be forgotten. The emotions cycling through me. Shocked, then sad. So deeply sad. Even angry.

Too soon. Far, far too soon. When is life enough? I guess (*hope*) that *enough* comes closer to my nineties. Maybe even later. We want forever, but we don't get forever.

We assume we have a tomorrow, but not necessarily.

Many great philosophers wrestled with the human condition of mortality. Marcus Aurelius said: "It is not death that a man should fear, but he should fear never beginning." Seneca said we shouldn't fear dying because it is always on our heels. Yesterday belongs to death.

Is death scary because of our unfinished lives? Because of that thing we always wanted to do and haven't? Because we didn't fully tend to our relationships the way we wanted?

> *"None of this stuff is really about morality or religion or dogma or big fancy questions of life after death.*
> *The capital-T Truth is about life BEFORE death.*
> *It is about the real value of a real education, which has almost nothing to do with knowledge, and everything to do with simple awareness; awareness of what is so real and essential, so hidden in plain sight all around us, all the time, that we have to keep reminding ourselves over and over:*
> *'This is water.'"*[19]

~ David Foster Wallace | *This Is Water*

Why put it off? Now is the best time to start.

Am I caring for my needs and those of others? Am I taking the time to cherish every moment? Do I tend to the important or trivial things with the proper amount of attention? Am I being curious and kind? Am I being my whole self and doing good things?

This is water.

Be curious, be kind, be whole, do good things.

Forty-One

Seeds

I played little league baseball for most of my youth. One year, my coach insisted we learn to eat sunflower seeds "the right way." We were doing it *wrong* by eating them one at a time. The right way meant loading up a cheek full of seeds. Work out one seed to crack and eat. Then move the empty shell to the other side. You could spit little pieces, but you weren't supposed to spit the shells until you cleared them all.

By the end of the season, most of us learned the proper way to eat sunflower seeds. Which meant I spent a lot of time with a cheek full of seeds practicing this necessary baseball skill. Three games into the season, I noticed I was getting on base more frequently. This was huge for me. I was a decent fielder, but never that productive at the plate. It finally dawned on me that every time I got on base, I had seeds in my cheek. The couple of times I didn't make it to base? That's right, no seeds. Coach was right. Learning to eat sunflower seeds correctly was monumental in advancing my, now-inevitable, pro-baseball career. As the great Michael Scott said: "I am not superstitious, but I am a little-stitious."

In hindsight, I never properly valued the facts that didn't support my story. If I got on base with seeds—proof! If I struck out without seeds—more proof! I paid little to no attention to when I struck out with a mouth full of seeds. This is human nature. We seek patterns to support our story. We blindly discard those that don't. This is both natural and common and it has a name: confirmation bias.

Our brain is wired to be hyper-efficient, so it builds shortcuts. These shortcuts are part of our brain. They are part of the System 1 thinking we learned at the beginning of the book. It is autopilot. The more we *know* something, the fiercer the confirmation bias is. The more thoughtful part of our brain, System 2, has to be pushed before there is any learning. I can challenge my deeply ingrained biases by seeking information from various sources. Especially those that differ from my current point of view.

Even with efforts to fight it, our brains will continue to enforce confirmation bias. If we focus on humility and curiosity, we will more likely have an open mind that allows us to see, rather than assume, what's really there.

What beliefs have I not questioned lately, or ever? Do I know others, or assume I do? How do I know when I am on autopilot? What would it take to change my mind?

Be curious, be kind, be whole, do good things.

Forty-Two

Lunch

I stood at the cafeteria's entrance in our forty-two-story office building, completely overwhelmed. It was my first day at a new company, my first big-time job. To say it wasn't going exactly how I expected was an understatement. Earlier that day, I accidentally triggered the security alarm and was greeted by armed security guards. When I finally found my floor, no one knew why I was there or where I was supposed to sit. I had survived until lunchtime and just wanted to eat a quiet lunch and rethink all of my life choices up to that point.

In the lunchroom, after purchasing food, a small door led to an unexpected and overwhelmingly large series of seating areas. I thought I knew what I was doing, but I didn't. I just needed a seat, but there were too many rooms and options. Holding my tray in the doorway, I stood frozen. I was trying to decide where to go, leaning toward setting my tray down and leaving. Maybe never coming back.

A group of guys called me over. I'd never seen them before, but they grabbed a fifth chair for their table of four and invited me to sit with them. Clearly, the table was uncomfortable with five, but they didn't seem to mind. We bonded at that lunch.

Much of my early success was because of the relationships created that day. I knew people in other departments who had unique experiences. That led to meeting other people. We were all able to help each other navigate the extensive machine. Those connections created opportunities for growth that were much larger than expected.

Life sometimes has us suddenly joining new ecosystems. When someone joins mine, I must prioritize making connections.

Can I connect with others? Am I inviting the new kid to lunch? Do I appreciate it is someone's first day?

Be curious, be kind, be whole, do good things.

Forty-Three

Detection

In the early 1900s, real mystery writers formed a club. Members of this group wrote *rules* that must be followed for *proper* mysteries. The rules included things like: the guilty party had to appear early in the story, no surprise twins, no more than one secret room or passage, and the stupid sidekick must only be slightly stupider than the average reader. The movie *Murder by Death* makes a point to break every one of those rules.[20]

> "Locked, from the inside. That can only mean one thing. And I don't know what it is."
>
> ~ Sam Diamond

If you decide to watch *Murder by Death*, you should know it is silly, but also culturally insensitive. The movie attacks every trope. An eccentric millionaire invites the top five detectives in his city to his murder-mystery party and whoever solves the murder gets one million dollars. The detectives are satirical versions of Sam Spade, Poirot, Miss Marple, and others from the Golden Age of mysteries. As they say, hilarity ensues.

Several members of The Detection Club, including Agatha Christie, set out to artfully break many of these *rules*. While others in the club faded into history, Agatha's stories continue to be popular. One of my favorite Agatha Christie novels is *The Murder of Roger Ackroyd*. This is a wonderfully enjoyable book that is celebrated by readers and critics, and she broke at least three of the ten rules. No spoilers on which rules.

Sometimes we see rules based on our perception and not on what things are or could be. Many times, the *rules* are not even really rules, they are just habits or routines. They rarely hold up to scrutiny. We need to find what works for us, even if it is a different approach.

Do I sufficiently question things that look like rules? Am I clear enough on intent to break those that need to be broken? Is there a better, more artful way to approach?

Be curious, be kind, be whole, do good things.

Forty-Four

Cake

"Hope and fear are two sides of the same coin: if we would be free of fear, we must let go of hope."

~ Sam Harris, Neuroscientist

I wrestle with this idea. I think I see where Sam Harris is coming from, but I also cling dearly to my hope. Writing about and discussing an idea helps me understand it more fully.

Sam is an instructor of mindfulness. Mindfulness has a common goal of accepting the present moment. He suggests that if we are living in fear or buried in hope, then we are insisting on a change. Hope, by its very nature, is intent on a different future. Whatever I might be afraid of, or hope for, is something that I am not currently happy with. This can impede accepting the current moment.

While floating this idea with some friends, they asked me, "Is that supposed to be the goal? To be in the present moment?"

I am not sure where I stand on this, but what I do know is *dessert*. Dessert is delicious. There isn't much that I don't like about a sweet treat. The beautiful thing about cake isn't having just eaten a big piece. It isn't about knowing that I might get to eat one in the future. The beautiful thing about a delicious piece of cake is slowly and carefully savoring each bite.

I think living a full and enjoyed life is about savoring and appreciating each bite. I may wish for a different type, more pieces, or something else. But I can still fully enjoy and appreciate what I currently have.

Have I tested my theories and beliefs? Is my focus on the future, or the past, obscuring my current moment? Am I pausing to acknowledge what I have? Will I savor this very moment?

Be curious, be kind, be whole, do good things.

Forty-Five

Kool-Aid

As a kid, we could feel in our bones when there were only two servings of Kool-Aid left in the pitcher. We'd put two glasses right next to each other and pour small amounts in each cup. Pouring smaller and smaller amounts, seeking perfect parity. This is the image I conjure when I hear "work-life" balance. Carefully ensuring that I've got a perfect balance between the work glass and the life glass.

I know it is a language shortcut to distinguish time on the job versus time off the job. But work and life are not two distinct things. These words are a little tricky. What is work? We work all the time. We tend to homes, have hobbies, take part in charitable efforts, and countless other ways.

In an average week, we might spend forty hours with our job. Assuming eight hours of sleep each night, that's another fifty-six. Are the remaining seventy-two hours what is called *life*?

Poet and author David Whyte says that we have "three marriages" in life to describe what we must tend to. The things we work on, ourselves, and our relationships.

> "Work-life balance is a concept that has us simply lashing ourselves on the back and working too hard in each of the three commitments. In the ensuing exhaustion, we ultimately give up on one or more of them to gain an easier life."
>
> ***
>
> "The current understanding of work-life balance is too simplistic. People find it hard to balance work with family, family with self, because it might not be a question of balance. Some other dynamic is in play, something to do with a very human attempt at happiness that does not quantify different parts of life and then set them against one another. We are collectively exhausted because of our inability to hold competing parts of ourselves together in a more integrated way."[21]
>
> ~ David Whyte | *The Three Marriages*

David uses *conversations* to describe the parts of living that require tugging and pulling to fit right. Conversations negotiate. They have multiple sides, with give and take. They require that we listen, consider, and inform. Conversations take turns, time, and thought.

Work-life balance is not about occasionally comparing the glasses of work and life. It is a conversation we should constantly nurture. I should tend to my work, self, and relationships. It's an ever-present shifting conversation between those three areas of my life that need my care.

Am I caring for myself? Have I tended to my relationships? Is my work accomplishing my goals? Which plant needs water right now? If I've been tended to, who around me could use help?

Be curious, be kind, be whole, do good things.

Forty-Six

Tacos

I love Jack in the Box tacos. Seasoned meat, American cheese, lettuce, and hot sauce stuffed into a corn tortilla, then deep-fried. Just add curly fries and a Dr. Pepper.

One night in college, a debate started about who could eat the most tacos. We pooled our money and bought all the tacos we could afford. It took three trays to carry the fifty tacos to our table. As we started, we realized we didn't have enough tacos for this stupid competition. We were out of money, but the staff had become emotionally invested and chipped in. All said and done, I won(?) with thirty-two tacos. Whatever you are picturing about the next few hours, it was worse. So. Much. Worse. It was at least a full day before I ate again. Maybe two days.

I did eat again, though. Hunger is much like exercise and sleep. I cannot eat one big meal and never eat again. I cannot have a long nap and never need to sleep again. Much of life is learning to moderate. Too little or too much can be disruptive. Unfortunately, I can have too much of something I love. I didn't have Jack in the Box tacos again for at least a decade.

Whether work, play, or rest, living life is finding balance. Not balance in the sense of equal parts of each at all times, but harmony. When we find the harmony, everything benefits. I must pay attention to my current state and adjust accordingly. I must know and tend to my needs.

Where, in my life, am I trying to eat one big meal, to never have to eat again? Am I balancing the conversation of work, play, and rest? Do I know what I need?

Be curious, be kind, be whole, do good things.

Forty-Seven

Rain

It was pouring rain early one morning as I drove into the office. The four lanes on my side of the highway had water pooling. I kept a safe following distance and avoided my lane neighbors. Ahead of me and two lanes to my right, I noticed something. *Were those headlights?* One lane to my right brightened with brake lights. It was headlights, and they were now in my lane, headed towards me.

A car had lost control and was spiraling across the four-lane highway, headed my direction. The car was moving unpredictably, so I didn't know the safe move. I was trying to check my rear view mirror, but was so afraid to take my eyes off of their car. I just slowed as much as I could, bracing for an impact from the front or the back. They came to a stop directly facing me. I was in shock and thankful that the car was no longer on a collision course with mine. Once stopped, they headed to the shoulder, and I safely went around them, slightly shaken for the rest of the morning.

This scary moment reminded me of a lesson I learned at seventeen years old. The weather was a wintry mix, which is a pleasant description of a bonkers combo of snow, ice, sleet, and torment. I was too close to the car ahead of me, but I was confident in my driving skills in a sports car that could stop on a dime. We crossed a bridge, and the van fish-tailed on ice before it slowed down. I hit my brakes. Nothing happened and I continued towards the van, a crash impending. I slowed down, but not fast enough. I was *very* lucky and stopped just before smashing the van. On that day, I learned brakes don't stop the car, they stop the wheels.

Sometimes I forget this and think that brakes stop the car. I think that I am being safe enough and I've sufficiently planned. My plans are often fair-weather plans. My plans involve everything happening according to either my best or second best-case scenario.

If I am walking on the edge of the cliff, there is no stumble room. Can I add a buffer? Am I depending on protective measures to do something they can't? Where can I be more thoughtful in planning? How could I be more prepared for unexpected events? Am I ready?

Be curious, be kind, be whole, do good things.

Forty-Eight

Hiking

As a Boy Scout, there are two patches coveted more than others. First is the polar bear award, a ten-minute swim in freezing weather. Second is the twenty-mile hike patch, a single-day twenty-mile trek with limited resting.

In this particular trip, we were aiming for the latter. We were a loud group of 40+ kids, so we rarely saw much non-scout wildlife. However, we watched beavers make a dam in a creek on this trip. We saw a few deer. It seemed like a perfect hike until the sky turned gray about ten miles in. It started sprinkling rain, which quickly turned torrential. The nearly dry creek rose rapidly, and we were suddenly waist-deep in water. As we scrambled to higher ground, we lost our paper map. Adults have this condition of talking to kids like they are kids. Once things turned serious, we all became equals. The tone shifted, and the expectations were high for the rest of this trip. We all grew up very quickly, and the adults engaged accordingly.

There was a point when we became so saturated with rain that we no longer cared to avoid the rain. *Wet* doesn't do justice to how soaked we were, and it was frigid. We were at the halfway point, so we had a decision to make. We didn't have the map, and the path we'd taken was underwater. We pressed forward and kept our eyes out for suitable shelter.

After walking another couple of hours through the rain, we finally found a hay barn. Our whole group jumped a barbed wire fence and made ourselves at home on someone's farm. Under different circumstances, we would have complained about the rickety barn, the itchy hay, or the bats hanging in it. But it was the most wonderful shelter we'd ever seen.

After the rain, we got back to the headquarters and looked at a fresh map. We estimated we had hiked about twenty-five miles. Once we got our patches, I used a Sharpie and ensured ours showed the full credit.

I cannot control the weather. It just happens. My perspective of that barn would have been very different had I seen it before the rain. Sometimes my only option is to keep walking. Sometimes I can find a barn. I may have options, but I cannot control the rain. So, worrying about the weather won't serve me.

Do I have or need a map? What if I lose it? Can I appreciate the barn? Am I wasting time being mad at the rain?

Be curious, be kind, be whole, do good things.

Forty-Nine

Giving Tree

"The baby bat
Screamed out in fright,
'Turn on the dark,
I'm afraid of the light.'"

~ Shel Silverstein | "Batty"

I read *The Giving Tree* by Shel Silverstein many times as a child, along with most of his other books. I love Shel's silliness for the sake of silliness, and sometimes there were more profound messages in the stories. *The Giving Tree* is about the relationship between an apple tree and its boy. The tree is very selfless and is always there for the boy, regardless of what he needs.

A joy of parenting is sharing beloved childhood treasures with your children. I recall when I pulled out *The Giving Tree* as an adult. I was excited to share the fun story and teach the virtue of selflessness. Yet, a deep sadness came over me as I read the story as a parent now. The story felt less about the tree's selflessness and more about the boy's selfishness and lack of gratitude. It reminded me of how important it is to set healthy boundaries. This tree could have provided many apples to many more kids. Instead, it gave *everything* to one boy and had nothing left to give.

Being selfless is an important virtue. Prioritizing self-care is an important virtue. I can give a lot but should make certain I have something left to give. As I reread that story, I saw it with different eyes. I cannot keep the view by taking the window. I cannot hold on to the past. It is gone, and I am a different person. I need to take care of others, take care of myself, and allow for growth in both.

Can I be selfless? Will I preserve healthy boundaries? Do I ensure I have enough to give another day?

Be curious, be kind, be whole, do good things.

Fifty

Impossible

In a small closet, I changed into a paper gown. My anxiety was at its peak as I got ready for an MRI. I'd never been claustrophobic until I stared into that plastic tube. I didn't want to do it, but my back pain had become intolerable. The doctor ordered scans of my neck and back.

I felt the closeness of the machine. I was proud of how well I did with the lower back scans. The machine felt like it was closing in on me, but it was almost over. It was noisy, and the room stank of sweat. In hindsight, that may have been me. I had made it to the last section. I had this in the bag. All was going acceptably until the technician said over the room speaker: "Don't swallow for the next minute."

Mission: Impossible.

I was certain my body started producing ten times the amount of saliva I needed. I became hyperaware of how much I needed to move my throat. He reminded me several times that he needed me to *not* swallow. I believe I wouldn't have moved at all had he not mentioned it. But, with all the attention and focus there, it suddenly became a problem.

Things become a very big deal when I place too much attention on them. Something that I normally wouldn't care about. Things that others wouldn't notice or care about. Taking a step back, and regaining a full view, helps me regain proper perspective.

Am I giving the situation enough attention? Is it too much attention? Should I step back and refocus?

Be curious, be kind, be whole, do good things.

Fifty-One

Oh Crap

I put the pro in procrastinating. I mastered the fine art of thirty minutes of work over eight hours, followed by eight hours of work in thirty minutes. Focusing takes tremendous effort, but once I am engaged, I can accomplish a tremendous amount. I want to be better; it is just so hard. I once read that *in order to change our habits, we need to change our environment*. I found this advice exceptionally useful. I still procrastinate, but I have adjusted my environment to help manage it. However, the book with the advice didn't phrase it that way. What the book actually said was, "Go commando."

I was reading *Oh Crap! Potty Training*. Why? I hosted a team meeting, where I had everyone pick a book, movie, or song. Many in that group suffer from a fear of public speaking. I asked them to share a book, movie, or song and then tell me why they picked it. Their presentation of their book, movie, or song went so smoothly. Everyone was eager to share their beloved item and why they selected it. We heard about songs they listened to with their grandparents and movies they watched with a parent. One person told about a song they heard on a first date with a person that became their spouse. Afterwards I pointed out that they had no problems with public speaking, so their fear must be tied to something else.

I didn't tell them upfront that I planned on reading, watching, and listening to the entire list. A recent mother picked the book she was reading at the time, so there I was, reading a potty training book with my youngest at nine years old.

I am delighted I read it. I found some sage advice. While the book coaches parents through their potty training woes, it is truly a book about how we learn. Here's a peek at some notes and expanding ideas I jotted down:

- Potty training is exciting because it is the first time we see how our children learn. [We all learn a little differently, and that is exciting.]

- Regression is normal. [We must measure our progress over a longer time than we desire.]

- When is more important than how. [Going partway now is better than a perfect plan that is never acted on.]

- Must be mentally prepared and have a "hard start date." [We'll never start if we don't get ready. The first step is always the hardest.]

- Create blocks of time. [Chunk larger or extensive work into bite-size pieces.]

- Watch for signals when communicating. [Listening isn't passive, and active listening isn't just hearing words.]

- Pushing too hard creates resistance. [The best motivation is internal. External motivation can drive people away.]

- Instead of nagging, create prompts and cues. [Find encouraging ways to prompt behavior change.][22]

Reading a potty training book when I wasn't potty training someone allowed me to see the broader lessons. It was a valuable reminder that lessons are everywhere if I am paying attention.

Things are always happening around/to me; am I using the opportunity to learn from them? Will I take a step back to see more? Can I acknowledge I am still run by the same mental equipment that motivates a two year old?

Be curious, be kind, be whole, do good things.

Fifty-Two

Diary

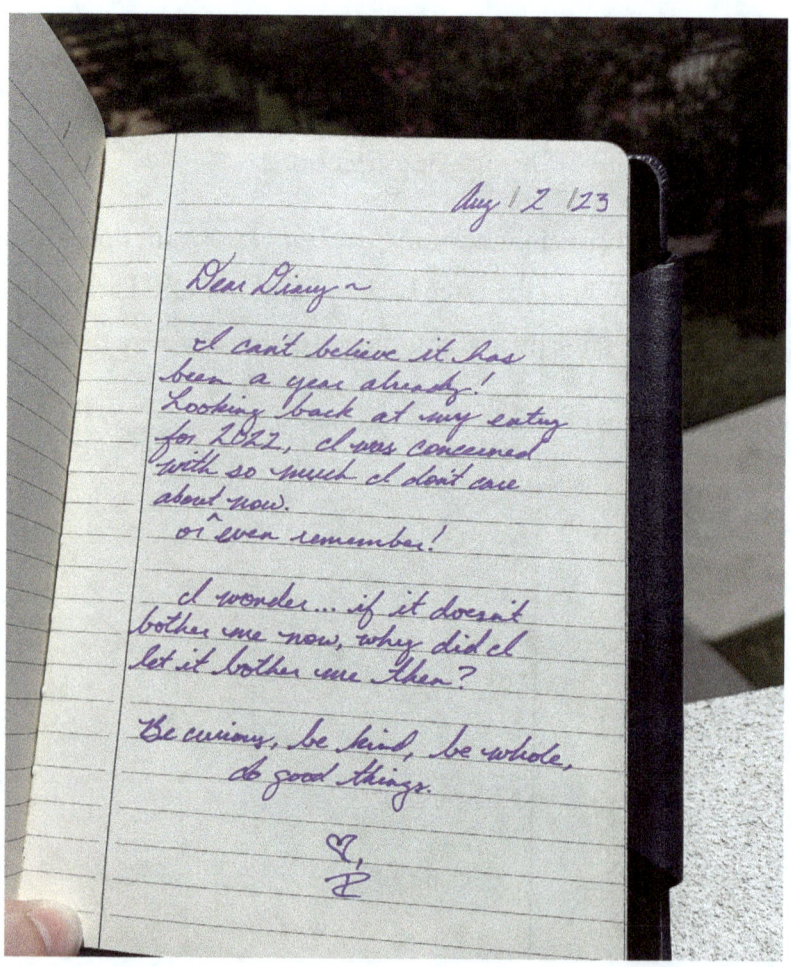

Aug 2 23

Dear Diary~

I can't believe it has been a year already! Looking back at my entry for 2022, I was concerned with so much I don't care about now, or even remember!

I wonder... if it doesn't bother me now, why did I let it bother me then?

Be curious, be kind, be whole, do good things.

(love),

R

PART THREE

My office job has taught me that everything we pitch needs a "So what?" to wrap up. Part Three is just that.

THE VOICE AND SILENCE OF OUR ATTENTION

The Voice

"We are all two people. One is standing behind us, whispering in our ear, comparing us. It is a voice in our head. And if anybody is thinking: 'What does he mean a voice in our head?' That's the voice that I mean!"

~ Benjamin Zander | paraphrased from "Work"

This *voice* acts as the playwright and director of the narrative of our life. My "other person" embellishes the past, making the good seem more focused on me and the bad seem more tragic. It also creates anxiety about a future going awry by conjuring different ways I might fail. He spends very little time in the *now* except to remind me when I am not measuring up to the story he's written for me. Sometimes his story is helpful. It can lead me to bigger goals or nudge me in a better direction. But it can also work against me by distracting or reminding me when I fall short or miss the mark. When this story is too narrow, too tightly scripted, I have no choice but to feel pain where life does not line up with it.

His play follows me, standing behind me like a shadow. Like my actual shadow, this one never quite lines up with reality. Sometimes it gets close, and I feel the excitement of that alignment. However, most of the time it is too far off, and I feel ashamed when I don't become what I am *supposed* to be. When I recognize my story isn't matching the director's plan, I feel guilty. This guilt compounds my desire to whip myself into shape. If left unchecked, I get pushed around from one plot point to the next, mindlessly milling through life.

My life is not his scripted play. I can't cast the various characters. I don't get to write lines for the other cast members. Failing to measure up to my director's story isn't a real failure. Sometimes my frustration with the behavior of others is simply them not complying with a script they know nothing about. Others are not working against me or out of place. They are just unaware of the part my playwright has written for them. There is no theater audience waiting for the flawless execution of the play. Instead, there is my own very real life, which includes my actions, reactions, and the people I share those moments with.

While my life is full of stories, life is not a story. I shouldn't try to send all experiences through a script rewrite. I should not be ashamed when life does not match the cues. Instead, I should tend to the moment based on my actual needs in that time. I must be present. To be fully present, I need to make room for myself and others. I should be responsible for where I am, not embarrassed by it. I can set goals and intentions, and I can work towards them, but I must leave room to live life. I must leave room to celebrate beauty, appreciate art, and know those around me. Know them for who they are, not the actors in my play. I must give them grace. Give myself grace. And breathe.

Pay Attention

"Pay attention to what you pay attention to."
~ Amy Krouse Rosenthal

I've had significant moments in my life that have led to drastic changes. I usually tie many of these moments to milestone events–like marriage, children, etc., but some of them come from small conversations. One of these conversations triggered a drastic shift when a kind friend told me I was becoming miserable to be around.

Naturally, I assumed my friend did not know what he was talking about. I thought I was being practical. Cynicism gave me the room to celebrate when other people were wrong. Of course, if they were right, I might still find some shortcoming to highlight. Despite assuming he was crazy, I paid very close attention to my interactions. As you have already assumed, he was right. I was a problem. I was a whiner who was infecting everyone around me. Simply put, I was self-absorbed and negative.

My sense of humor leans to sarcasm, and my personality bends toward cynicism. These, combined with an overly inward point of view, had poisoned my worldview. I declared every project a failure from the beginning. I felt like I was overworked, underappreciated, and surrounded by idiots.

As a self-proclaimed *realist*, I was on a mission to point out the flaws in everything. All venting had deteriorated into pure complaining. Nothing would be good enough, no one could do anything right, and I was all too ready to point it out to anyone unfortunate enough to be around me. I didn't even realize just how miserable I had become. Complaining became a habit. Even if something wasn't that bad, I pulled out a fine-toothed comb to uncover the worst parts.

It took a while and still requires effort, but I developed a new perspective. I learned I am pessimistic when I pay attention to the negatives in life. I am happiest and most successful when I focus on understanding and compassion. The literal root of the word "understand" is "to stand in the midst of" and the word "compassion" stems from the concept of "suffering together." As I have immersed myself amid others and shared in the togetherness of our joint issues, I found a tremendous change in my attitude, outlook, and perception of my work.

When I complain, feel targeted, or become miserable, I remind myself:

1. Before I react, I must seek to understand the circumstances (be curious)
2. I should assume the best intentions from others (be kind)
3. Together we achieve more when we bring everything (be whole)
4. Complaining doesn't help–be the change I want to see (do good things)

We invest our attention in the immediate things like phone notifications and emails, but we are defined by what we do and how we contribute to the long-term.

THE ANTIDOTE

Two thoughts to set the tone. The first is from Anne Lamott's book on writing and life, *Bird by Bird*.

> "E. L. Doctorow said once said that, 'Writing a novel is like driving a car at night. You can see only as far as your headlights, but you can make the whole trip that way.' You don't have to see where you're going, you don't have to see your destination or everything you will pass along the way. You just have to see two or three feet ahead of you. This is right up there with the best advice on writing, or life, I have ever heard."

The second is from David Foster Wallace's *This Is Water*.

> "There are these two young fish swimming along, and they happen to meet an older fish swimming the other way, who nods at them and says:
> *'Morning, boys. How's the water?'*
> And the two young fish swim on for a bit, and then eventually

one of them looks over at the other and goes: '*What the hell is water?*'"

I'll reassure you, as David does, "If you're worried that I plan to present myself here as the wise, older fish explaining what water is to you younger fish, please don't be. I am not the wise old fish. The point of the fish story is merely that the most obvious, important realities are often the ones that are hardest to see and talk about."

In various forms, *water* surrounds us constantly. It is ever-present and slowly fades into the background until it quietly disappears, if we even noticed it in the first place. It's the interactions with strangers and loved ones and our art, our work, and our rest. *Water* is a mundane trip to the grocery store, sitting in a meeting that doesn't seem relevant, or any other interaction as we move towards our destinations. I miss the water because I have autopilot engaged, or I am being too inwardly focused. Wallace consoles us by pointing out that we, of course, do this. Every single thought and memory we have is with ourselves at the very center of it.

When I am alert and actively paying attention to my surroundings, my headlights work better. I may still only see a few feet ahead of me, but that is good enough to move in the right direction. Moving can lead to forward momentum, making each of the next steps easier.

I practice meditation, specifically mindfulness. It helps me to acknowledge my thoughts and feelings for what they are. It helps me to release them as soon as they are no longer helpful. The intention is to observe without reacting. I practice using two different tools and teachers. Andy Puddicombe at *Headspace* is gentle and calming, and at the other end of the spectrum Sam Harris at *Waking Up* tries to melt your brain.

Sam Harris on meditation:

> "The goal of meditation is to uncover a form of well-being that is inherent to the nature of our minds. It must, therefore, be available in the context of ordinary sights, sounds, sensations, and even thoughts. Peak experiences are fine, but real freedom must be coincident with normal waking life."

> "Mindfulness is simply a state of open, nonjudgmental, and nondiscursive attention to the contents of consciousness, whether pleasant or unpleasant."[23]

Andy Puddicombe on noting:

> "Noting is a very interesting technique and often much misunderstood. It is tempting to think that we have to be on guard the whole time, trying to catch every single thought. In that moment of awareness, the moment we realize we've been distracted, we use the noting to create a bit of space, as a way of letting go, and to gain some clarity and learn more about our habits, tendencies, and conditioning. But noting can only happen when awareness is present. By definition, we cannot be both distracted and aware at the same time."[24]

In *This Is Water*, David Foster Wallace says:

"You get to consciously decide what has meaning and what doesn't. You get to decide what to worship.

The capital-T Truth is about life BEFORE death. It is about the real value of a real education, which has almost nothing to do with knowledge, and everything to do with simple awareness; awareness of what is so real and essential, so hidden in plain sight all around us, all the time, that we have to keep reminding ourselves over and over: 'This is water.' 'This is water.' It is unimaginably hard to do this, to stay conscious and alive in the adult world day in and day out. This means yet another grand cliché turns out to be true: your education really IS the job of a lifetime. And it commences: now. I wish you way more than luck."[25]

Mindfulness is the alarm that alerts me to the water.

Tame the voice in your head. Find comfort in *who* you are. Pay attention. And pay attention to what you pay attention to. Find comfort in *where* you are. This is water.

Can I increase my awareness to better notice, and appreciate, my surroundings? Can I reduce my busyness to slow down, or wake up, to ensure I am absorbing the rich texture of life? How can I more purposefully engage in what I am doing?

Be curious, be kind, be whole, do good things.

Acknowledgments

"In a disagreement about art, whoever likes it is right."
~ Teller (paraphrased by Penn)

Thank you to my parents for my weird childhood and for encouraging me to be curious about whatever I wanted. This includes supporting my dozens of rotating hobbies. My dad always encouraged me to appreciate art that I didn't understand. He also suggested I just like what I like, regardless of popularity. Whoever likes the art is right.

Thank you to Robin and our kids for accepting my increasingly peculiar tendencies when I am writing, reading, or testing new thoughts. I am grateful for their patience and for letting me share (my version of) our stories. Thank you to Eva for the use of her artwork.

Thank you to Staci and Sara for guiding me through many edits.

Apologies to family, friends, their parents, and colleagues who may recognize our stories here. I hope I got at least as much right as wrong. If you've taken offense to anything, please let me know. However, I will only accept submitted complaints in the form of you writing your own book.

ACKNOWLEDGMENTS

INFLUENCES

Michael Weber said that influence is "honestly revealing what matters most to you is in a way what gives others the opportunity to see an intersection point for themselves." This intersection is where your path crosses theirs, and you might find an opportunity to move the common work forward.

> "You should have read all the good stuff so that you know what has been done, because if you have a story like one somebody else has written, yours isn't any good unless you can write a better one. In any art you're allowed to steal anything if you can make it better, but the tendency should always be upward instead of down. And don't ever imitate anybody. All style is, is the awkwardness of a writer in stating a fact. If you have a way of your own, you are fortunate, but if you try to write like somebody else, you'll have the awkwardness of the other writer as well as your own."
>
> ~ Ernest Hemingway

I hope you enjoy the awkwardness of these creators' efforts, as they are the artists who have contributed to my foundation. Check in and let me know what you think of their stuff, and share with me who has influenced you.

INFLUENCES

Scan the QR code go to the link to see my list of influences. https://rli.icu/grow

I've collected all of the references, links, and end notes in the book at https://richardingram.me/bimow-references/ or scan the QR code below

1. "The Breaking of the Wand with magician Michael Weber." Jesse's Office. July 31, 2019. Video, https://rli.icu/1.

2. Saxe, John Godfrey. "The Blind Man and the Elephant." The Poems of John Godfrey Saxe. Boston: Ticknor and Fields. 1872. p. 259-261. All spelling and cultural depictions are consistent with the original text but may be insensitive to some readers.

3. Hanson, Dr. Rick. "Pet the Lizard." Rick Hanson, Ph.D. https://rli.icu/liz.

4. Hanson, Dr. Rick. "Feed the Mouse." Rick Hanson, Ph.D. https://rli.icu/mou.

5. Hanson, Dr. Rick. "Hug the Monkey." Rick Hanson, Ph.D. https://rli.icu/mon.

6. "12 truths I learned from life and writing." TED2017. April 2017. Video, https://rli.icu/d.

7. "Eyewitness Identification Reform in Arkansas." Innocence Project, April 28, 2023. https://rli.icu/6.

8. Sheldon, Robert, and Ivy Wigmore. "What Is Availability Bias – TechTarget Definition." WhatIs.com, November 7, 2022. https://rli.icu/7.

9. Statista Research Department. "Number of police-reported fatal vehicle crashes in the United States from 1993 to 2020." Statista.com, November 2, 2022. https://rli.icu/5.

10. Statista Research Department. "Number of unprovoked shark attacks worldwide from 2000 – 2022." Statista.com, March 31, 2023. https://rli.icu/2.

11. Statista Research Department. "Number of worldwide air traffic fatalities from 2006 to 2021." Statista.com, March 1, 2022. https://rli.icu/3.

12. Statista Research Department. "Number of lives lost due to tornadoes in the United States from 1995 to 2021." Statista.com, June 2022. https://rli.icu/4.

13. "Start with Why—how Great Leaders Inspire Action." TEDx Talks. September 28, 2009. Video, https://rli.icu/why.

14. Godin, Seth. "Blunders and Mistakes." Seth's Blog, December 17, 2020. https://rli.icu/8.

15. Ross, Loretta J. "Don't Call People Out—Call Them In." Loretta J. Ross: Don't call people out—call them in, August 2021. Video, https://rli.icu/9.

16. "Family Answers" Public Service Announcement, 1996. Adapted.

17. Talavera, Karen. "Carrot, Egg or Coffee: Which Are You?" November 29, 2011. https://rli.icu/a. Adapted.

18. Van Hare, Holly. "Quaker Oats boast 35 percent less sugar, actually just smaller packet" October 20, 2017. https://rli.icu/b.

19. Foster Wallace, David. "Your Mind Is an Excellent Servant, but a Terrible Master - David Foster Wallace." YouTube, January 28, 2020. https://rli.icu/dfw.

20. From the Introduction to The Best Detective Stories of 1928–29. Reprinted in Haycraft, Howard. *Murder for Pleasure: The Life and Times of the Detective Story.* Revised edition. New York. Biblio and Tannen. 1976.

21. Whyte, David. *The Three Marriages: Reimagining Work, Self, and Relationship.* New York: Riverhead Books, 2010.

22. Glowacki, Jamie. *Oh Crap! Potty Training: Everything Modern Parents Need to Know to Do It Once and Do It Right.* New York: Gallery Books, 2019.

23. Harris, Sam. *Waking Up: A Guide to Spirituality Without Religion.* New York: Simon & Schuster Paperbacks, 2015.

24. Puddicombe, Andy. "What the Noting Technique Is, and How to Take Advantage of it Andy." Headspace. Accessed August 18, 2023. https://rli.icu/c.

25. Wallace, David Foster. *This Is Water.* New York: Little, Brown, 2009.

www.ingramcontent.com/pod-product-compliance
Lightning Source LLC
LaVergne TN
LVHW021117080426
835512LV00011B/2549